OF TRIBES AND TRIBULATIONS

OF TRIBES AND TRIBULATIONS

KENNETH D. ROSEMAN

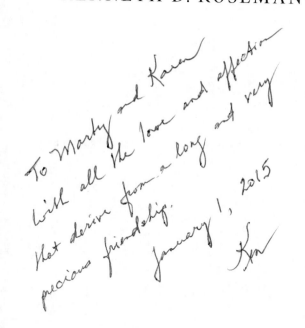

To Marty and Karen
with all the love and affection
that derive from a long and very
precious friendship.
January 1, 2015
Ken

WIPF & STOCK · Eugene, Oregon

OF TRIBES AND TRIBULATIONS

Wipf and Stock
An Imprint of Wipf and Stock Publishers
199 W. 8th Ave., Suite 3
Eugene, OR 97401

www.wipfandstock.com

ISBN 13: 978-1-4982-0046-2

Manufactured in the U.S.A.   10/29/2014

Contents

Appreciation

THE IDEAS EXPRESSED IN these essays have been developed gradually over the past fifty-three years. They were born, usually unexpectedly, in conversations, readings, classes, and a host of experiences. It would be almost impossible to specify the precise genesis of each thought, but I express a general sense of gratitude for everyone whose influence has found its way onto these pages.

Of particular note, however, has been the stimulation of "Torah Class" students in Madison, WI, Dallas, TX, and Corpus Christi, TX, as well as students in classes I have taught at Southern Methodist University and Texas A&M University-Corpus Christi. Invariably, one or more of them would pose a penetrating question that forced me to think about the "tribulations" of this book in new and better ways.

In my profession, three men stand out as early formative influences, and I owe a deep debt of gratitude to each one. Rabbi Balfour Brickner was the rabbi I was close to during my teenage years and the first person who directed me into a rabbinic career. Dr. Nelson Glueck was President of Hebrew Union College-Jewish Institute of Religion. He took a chance by appointing a newly ordained rabbi to a position of considerable authority on the seminary faculty, and I hope this book demonstrates that his trust was not misplaced. Dr. Jacob Rader Marcus guided me both professionally and academically over many years. I am intensely appreciative of his mentoring, counsel, and friendship.

The manuscript of this book has been greatly improved by the careful and thoughtful critique of my colleague, Rabbi Samuel Stahl of San Antonio, TX. While I am ultimately responsible for the volume's contents, Sam made me think and rethink what I wanted to write, and the book is inevitably better because of him.

My most profound thanks, however, are directed to my father, Alvin Jerome (aka Isaac) Roseman. He has been absent from our lives for over forty years, yet his influence is ever-present. He was the best teacher I ever had. In high school, I would sit with him on the couch in our Washington, DC living room and painstakingly go over my written work with him. The white paper often looked like the Blood Mobile had suffered a catastrophic accident, but the copious red marks and his patient explanations taught me the value of clarity of expression, precise use of language, and the imperative of organizing one's thoughts carefully.

This book, then, is as much his legacy as mine, and it is lovingly dedicated to his memory.

Introduction

Who, What, Why: A Rationale

THIS IS NOT AN autobiography and certainly not a chronological annal for the last fifty-some years. You would undoubtedly be bored to tears by such a recital, and I dread the idea of having to do it. There will surely be anecdotes that enter into my narratives, but the focus will be on a thematic statement of what I have tried to do during my career, what I think my own values were, and both what I disdained and what I held dear. Because this is not intended as an academic work, references to sources and footnotes have been deliberately minimized.

Having said all that, however, it seems that a bit of personal background might serve to establish the context for what I shall say in these essays. Here, then, is the briefest sketch of my formative years. I was born in Washington, DC, the son of two Jewish parents. My father was an attorney (Western Reserve) and a social work administrator (Chicago). My mother was a graduate of Goucher College, but primarily a housewife and communal volunteer. Both were liberal Democrats, and our home in DC was often full of similarly minded people, like Joseph Rauh, head of the Americans for Democratic Action. My father worked for the Roosevelt administration, first in the Social Security Administration, and then in the Office of the President, where he oversaw relief activities for those displaced within the U.S. by the Great Depression. During WWII, he was stationed in Cairo with the British Army, where he was responsible for refugee planning, specifically how to save the many Europeans in the area should the German army have won at El Alamein. After the war, he continued administering international projects of human assistance, either with the United Nations or with the foreign aid programs funded by the U.S. government. As children, my sister and I lived with our parents in DC, but also in Greece, Switzerland, and Cambodia. My sister also spent a year in the Philippines. During our college years, our parents moved to Paris, France.

There were several consequences of this unusual upbringing. My sister resented the constant moving and her inability to establish friendships and roots, the normal routine of a teenage girl. I understand that reaction, since neither of us has any friends from before college graduation; we learned how to survive on our own and to keep attachments tentative and fluid. In that sense, we were like the children of military families, whose duty posts took them from one base to another, often with only minimal opportunity to say "good-bye" or make lasting new commitments. On the other hand, I felt especially privileged to have the experiences of foreign travel and living. I relished the years of school in Geneva and have actually rekindled some relationships with then-adolescents who were my classmates some sixty years ago. I particularly enjoyed the lessons Dad provided as we traveled the world. He was perhaps the best teacher I have ever known. When we drove through northern France, we learned the story of Joan of Arc; crossing the Alps, we were accompanied by Hannibal and his elephants; at the Chateau de Chillon in Montreux, he read us "The Prisoner of Chillon" by Byron. For my twelfth birthday, he took me to London and Cambridge, where we explored the Tower, Henry the VIII, Thomas More, and a host of other luminaries. In all, he kindled within me a lifelong passion for history and language. My happy memories also include such important dinner guests in our home as Eleanor Roosevelt and Abba Eban, and Edith Piaf entertaining at a diplomatic soiree in our living room. I was old enough to watch through the banister, but my sister was just enough younger that she missed the excitement.

Our Jewish education was necessarily constricted. Both of my parents grew up in Classical Reform Jewish homes, where Judaism was openly acknowledged, but as an ethical and moral imperative rather than a ritual practice. My grandmother was confirmed at Sinai Congregation in Chicago under Rabbi Emil G. Hirsch, and mother followed under the tutelage of Dr. Louis Mann. Those were days of Sunday Sabbath services, anti-Zionism, avoidance of Hebrew and (God forbid) Yiddish, militant assimilation, but also pioneering efforts in social service to the less-fortunate and the immigrant. Father's parents emigrated from Galicia (the Carpathian Mountain region of today's Slovakia) and eventually settled in Cleveland where they raised four children to be model Americans. To be sure, they gave each child a Jewish middle name, but those quickly were converted into American equivalents: Father's Isaac soon became Jerome and one of his brothers exchanged Leibl for Lincoln. From both sides of the family, universalism and Americanism rained. My maternal grandmother never quite understood why her grandson would dedicate his life to the Jewish sub-group of society. While I was at HUC-JIR, she repeatedly reminded me that, "when you're through with this phase, there will be a place in the family business for you." After I was ordained, the pyrrhic reassurance was replaced: "Are you still happy?" It was the same thing. Her offer was not especially enticing, since building steel-reinforced concrete retaining walls never appealed to me, and the business had been sold in 1947! I am pretty sure that my Classical Reform Jewish grandmother would be whirling in her tomb if she knew that her grandson was leading all-Hebrew traditional services every Shabbat morning, clad in kippah and tallit.

Overseas as a child, there was neither motivation nor opportunity to have a Jewish education. When I was twelve and might have been studying for my Bar Mitzvah, we were living in Athens. There was little family background to encourage this rite of passage, so there was never any serious consideration of Bar Mitzvah. In addition, that was not what a liberal Reform Jew did in the early 1950s. Besides, the only teacher who might have been available was a Sephardic rabbi who spoke no English and who had absolutely no idea of what an American adolescent or a liberal Jew was.

When we returned to the U.S. in 1953, I was lucky enough to have three sequential years in high school. (My sister had three different high school experiences between fifteen and eighteen, so her negative reaction to her upbringing is altogether understandable.) During those years, however, I was exposed to Rabbi Balfour Brickner, recently ordained from the Hebrew Union College-Jewish Institute of Religion in Cincinnati and just turning thirty years of age. Temple Sinai had no building, so we gathered every Friday night in the Bethlehem Chapel of the Washington National Cathedral. I was enlisted as the "shamash" or sexton, and I would arrive a half hour before services to slide the footlocker from under the pews, cover the crucifix, put out various ritual paraphernalia and make the space ready for the heathen invasion. I became president of the youth group, went to Jewish summer camp in Pennsylvania and Wisconsin, and was one of four in the first confirmation class of the congregation. It was both my first and my only significant exposure to Jewish life.

Rabbi Brickner and I stayed in touch. As my parents lived out of the country during my college years, I occasionally returned to Washington during vacations and bummed a room from a family friend. During the summer between my sophomore and junior years at Oberlin College, I had lunch with "Brick" one day in DC, and he asked me what I planned to do with my life. I could only tell him with conviction that I needed some career that would be intellectually stimulating and that would put me in frequent contact with people. There were many avenues through which I could satisfy these dual ambitions, but no one burning passion. He reached across the lunch table, grabbed me by the lapel and erupted: "You idiot! Don't you see? It's as plain as that big nose on your face. You can have everything you want in the rabbinate. You've got to consider that as a career." That was in 1959. The rest, as they say, is history. I went back to Oberlin, took a course in Jewish history, got hooked, and eventually enrolled at HUC-JIR.

In the winter of 1965-66, two things happened. First, the College-Institute registrar called me in and asked me to provide information for the calligraphy of my ordination certificate. Among the data requested was my Hebrew name, including my father's Hebrew name. In 1966, we were not yet including the mother's name. My own name was simple. Kenneth is as Scottish as it comes and, besides, the only "K" or hard "C" name in the Bible is Cain and I was not about to be named after the world's first murderer. But my middle name is David and that was perfectly acceptable. But I had no idea if my father had ever received a Hebrew name. So, despite his slight size (5'8" tall, 160 pounds), I assigned him the name *Aryeh*, which means "Lion." And that's how the ordination certificate reads. A dozen years later, after his death, I requested his personnel file from the State Department under the Freedom of Information Act. My father had always been known as Alvin Jerome Roseman, but, in an FBI security clearance review that I received through this request, I learned that his actual middle name was Isaac. He had changed it, apparently, because Isaac was too Jewish, given the rampant anti-Semitism in the government agencies for which he proposed to work. It was immediately obvious that Isaac was his true middle name. I was facing an identity crisis. (His youngest brother, who was named Monroe Lincoln, later told me that he had also changed his middle name from Leibl.) My mother was another story. Given her German-Jewish heritage, she would never have been blessed with a Hebrew name. Her English name was Edith. In 1987, a group of us were studying the eighteenth chapter of Genesis one Shabbat morning at Temple Shalom in Dallas. Someone asked what Lot's wife's name was. Our consensus was "Mrs." But I was curious and began reading in every volume of midrash I could find. In a source I can no longer locate, I discovered that Lot's wife was named *Idit* (*aleph-yod-dalet-yod-tof*). I broke out in laughter. Idit had to be the Hebrew for Edith, and my mother was so curious that she too would have looked back at Sodom and would still be standing in the Rift Valley as a pillar of salt. It was too perfect. I then converted Roseman into its Hebrew equivalent, *Vardi* (based on the word, *vered*, "rose"), leading finally to my completely reconfigured Hebrew name: *HaRav David Vardi ben Yitzhak ve-Idit*.

The second thing I was thinking was where I would end up after ordination that next June. Rabbi Roland B. Gittelsohn of Temple Israel in Boston simply assumed that I, as the top student in the class, would leap at the chance to become his assistant. Gittelsohn had been born in the house next door to my father, about six weeks later. The two boys grew up as inseparable friends, only to move in different directions during college years. He stayed at our home in Washington when he returned from Iwo Jima, having delivered a brilliant, though controversial, dedicatory sermon at the Marine Corps cemetery on that island. I wondered if I would be evaluated for myself or because I was Alvin Roseman's son. Right at that moment, an offer was extended to me by Dr. Nelson Glueck, president of the seminary, to become assistant dean and to continue in graduate school towards a doctoral degree. Gittelsohn was furious that I did not come to Boston, though he later understood and accepted my reasoning for staying in Cincinnati. Then, to my immense surprise, Dr. Samuel Sandmel, who was then serving as provost/dean of the school, decided to retire from administration and return to full-time teaching, leaving me even before ordination as assistant to myself. Only in retrospect did I appreciate the absurdity of being the academic head of a school from which I was just about to graduate. I should have fled to Boston or anywhere else. But in a moment of incredible naivete, I stayed in the job, and, for reasons I still don't completely comprehend, Glueck supported me, made me acting dean two years later and dean in 1970. In 1974, I left the College-Institute when then new president, Alfred Gottschalk and I were simply not on the same page, and moved to Rye, NY. For two years, I served as Director of the Institute for Jewish Life, then moved to congregations in Madison, Wisconsin, Dallas, Texas, and finally Corpus Christi, Texas.

My background, personality and principal approach to religion, in general, and to Judaism, in particular, has tended toward the rationalistic end of the spectrum. I have tried to understand this field of human interest and endeavor in the context of larger social and cultural influences and trends. Religious belief and practice are, to my way of thinking, symbiotically linked to both the historical circumstances from which they emerged and to the contemporary milieu in which they are manifest. Creative and innovative insight does not often arise from the intuition of brand-new facts, but from the recombination of existent data and ideas in ways that repattern our apprehension of reality.

No one has ever accused me of being a mystic, and only rarely have I thought of myself in that guise. Nonetheless, there have been moments when non-rational perceptions have deeply moved me. I'll speak more of this in the essay on Torah, but let me here recount only one example. I can hardly ever stand on the pulpit on a Friday evening, look down the center aisle of the sanctuary and sing the verse of *L'cha Dodi* that welcomes the Sabbath Bride without visualizing my own daughter in her wedding dress. An occasional experience of this sort has not made me a mystic, but it does serve as a cautionary limit to the relevance of rationality.

I have been married twice, both times happily. My first wife, Helen Hoodin, and I met in Cincinnati, married in December 1962, and continued for the next 32 ½ years until she died of breast cancer in 1995. In 1996, I married Phyllis Rubin Katz, and we continue as a couple until this day.

Can I hazard an evaluation of the last half-century? Like any career, there have been ups and downs. It was certainly not pleasant to be told that I was being relieved of my post at the College-Institute, just two weeks after my father had dropped dead of a heart attack. But even that setback turned out to be fortuitous, since I found a great job almost immediately and now look back on leaving Cincinnati as one of the best professional and personal things that ever happened to me. Had I stayed there, I suspect I would have become very provincial and limited in outlook; being forced out into a larger arena, I grew far more than I would have in the purely academic milieu. I suppose I could have earned more money in some other profession, but the coins with which I have been paid over the years are of immensely greater value than any mere monetary compensation could equal. I have had two good marriages, two wonderful children of my own and two marvelous daughters by marriage, four superb partners for the four children, eleven grandchildren and the satisfaction of living long enough to experience the joys of a growing, maturing, and achieving family of responsible and decent adults, something that neither of my own parents had the privilege of knowing, since they both died in their early sixties.

I am particularly indebted to Corpus Christi where I have served twelve years after failing miserably in my first attempt at retirement. (Phyllis says it lasted only twenty minutes!) It has been a wonderful place to conclude my career; a congregation that has allowed me to focus on those activities that originally attracted me into the rabbinate has saved me from the politics and "administrivia" involved in bigger congregations and a community that has honored me with worthwhile avenues of public service and so many wonderful friends that, like the promise to Abraham, they are "as numerous as the stars in the heaven."

One more word before we turn to the "tribes" and the "tribulations." I chose the second part of the title because, to be sure, not everything has been smooth sailing over the last five decades. There have been challenges and disappointments and certainly questions that have perplexed and nagged at me throughout the years. Any honest retrospective has to confront those issues honestly and forthrightly.

I wanted to use the word "tribes" for several different reasons. There were twelve tribes in biblical Israel and Judah. These were no abstractions, but shorthand ways of saying that there were real people involved in real life quests. My interest in history has led me to think of history as the record of how people, in specific times and circumstances, solved the problems of their daily lives. It has always been the human dimension of society that has fascinated me, so starting with tribes and continuing with their descendants seemed natural and easy. A second consideration. When I was a student at Ecole Privat in Geneva, we wore uniforms and by some chance I was assigned the number twelve. Since then, the number has had a special attraction for me, so the coincidence of that number with its biblical predecessor made the selection of twelve tribes inescapable.

I suppose that members of other professions have their own issues that they would term "tribulations." Never having been in another profession, I can only assume that this must be true, but I believe that there is something distinct about being a clergyperson that intensifies the issues and makes them more poignant. For one thing, the very nature of being in the clergy means that one is called to deal with intellectual and spiritual issues. Some clergy, under the press of daily obligations or due to predilections of personality, try to glide by this confrontation. But, truth to tell, you can elide, but you cannot hide. They are inescapable, at least in the long run. Further, because we confront these issues on a daily basis what could to others remain abstract, objective and at arm's length becomes for us deeply personal. And, even more, we are constantly the focus of demands by congregants and other to provide answers and substantive guidance to issues and tribulations that may be peripheral to their lives, but which are central to us.

I have undertaken this project with two ends in mind. After a rather lengthy career, it seems fitting and, perhaps, useful to reflect on the meanings, challenges, and values that I have confronted and with which I have wrestled, usually in private, but occasionally from the pulpit, in the classroom or in print. Socrates (Plato, *Apology* 38a) taught that "the unexamined life is not worth living." I am neither a world-altering philosopher nor do I have a particular taste for hemlock, but I am motivated by the wisdom of the sage of Athens as much as I am by the imperatives of Amos and Isaiah.

It may be helpful at the outset if I define what I mean by "religion." Many people equate religion with a combination of rituals, beliefs and behaviors. From this perspective, the Jewish religion is expressed (as one example) by the erection of a sukkah five days after Yom Kippur; by the recital of prayers that speak of gratitude to God for the bounty of the harvest; and by the implementation of this belief in acts of ecological responsibility. One might characterize this view of religion as a "substantive" definition. It is not a definition to which I subscribe.

Over the last fifty-five years, I have studied and observed a spectrum of world religions, and I have chosen and practiced one—liberal Judaism. I have come to believe in a "functional" definition of religion, much influenced by sociological theorists like Emile Durkheim. A functional definition proposes that religion in general fulfills an important function in human life. All of my study and experience leads me to the conclusion that the function that religion performs is to provide a *Weltanschauung*, a worldview, guidance for and perspective on life. This outlook on human existence derives from five questions that are, so far as I can ascertain, common to every one of the world's religions.

These are the questions:

1. What does it mean to be an individual human person? Am I created or simply an incidental and accidental fleck of matter? Am I at base sinful or good? I am convinced that all religion begins, not as one might imagine with God, but with an examination of the single, irreducible human being.

2. The second question derives naturally from the first. What should be the relationship between one individual and another? Under this rubric, we deal with ethics and morality, mutual obligations, and responsibilities.

3. Many people might miss the next question, but all religions deal with the physical universe. Was it created or, as in the philosophy of Aristotle, is matter eternal? Religions ask whether the world is real, or real only as an antecedent of the "real" real world of eternity, or simply as a mental construct based on direct sense perception. Religions also ask if people have an obligation "to tend and to till" the world (Gen 2:15) or if we are free to use and abuse it at will.

4. Religions ask whether there is a power beyond us. Many call this power God or Jesus or Allah, but it could equally be understood as Kismet or fate or the historical dynamic (as in the "religion" of Communism) or some other impersonal forces that surround us. We want to know if and how this power and humans communicate with each other. Are there duties that people have in relation to this power, and are there reciprocal obligations that this power has to us? And, as important as anything else, does our connection with this power continue after we die and in what manner?

5. Finally, if all the answers to questions 1-4 are significant, how do we put them into actual practice? This question involves social structures, rituals, government, schools, and other institutions in their exercise of power, authority, education and leadership and the consolidation of core values in canonic texts so that the principles of the faith may be shared across geographic space and chronological distance with minimal distortion.

All religions ask these questions. The questions are identical. Individual religions are separated because they answer the questions in different ways. And individual people affiliate with distinct religions because they find that the specific answers that one religion provides function better in their lives than other alternatives. (To be sure, family heritage and social, business, and political considerations play a role in any choice, but ultimately the religion's answers have to function effectively in one's life and make sense of the world if they are to have an effective impact in a person's life.)

Liberal Judaism for me combines a historical rootedness, including teachings that are often valid and meaningful in my life, rituals that express important values and truths, a flexible approach that empowers me as a person who has a right to make significant choices about my religious practices and beliefs, and, perhaps most significant, a purpose that organizes and directs my daily life. (More on this when we deal with "Covenant.")

When I first stood in the Chapel at HUC-JIR in Cincinnati and read what was inscribed on the proscenium arch over the ark, the sentence struck me as a guiding principle for my rabbinate. Rabbi Judah the Prince said *Veda lifnei mi atah omed* [*b. Berachot* 28b], which means "know before Whom you stand." In its original context, this adage meant that we should be aware that all one's actions are perceived by an all-knowing God Who will hold us accountable either in this life or the next. As a modern and liberal Jew, I choose to reinterpret this saying in multiple and alternative dimensions.

I stand before God. Not a judgmental God, but a God who created this world and so many of the boons that enrich my daily life—fertile soil, water, oxygen, other people I cherish, natural beauty and regularity—so much that preceded my existence and which form the ground of my life. As a creature in this world for the existence of which I had no role or responsibility, my stance must be one of gratitude and, even more, humility. I am the created, not the creator, and as a consequence, when I stand before God it is incumbent upon me to be intensely aware of that relationship and its implications.

I stand before the history of the Jewish people. To know the glorious contributions our people have made to world civilization evokes a response of pride. I am a child of a tradition that taught the world about a single deity whose actions were conditioned by the exalted ethics conveyed through the biblical prophets. I come from a two-thousand-year history of intellectual striving, a tradition that empowered human beings to use their mental capacity to elucidate the will of God rather than wait passively for a celestial revelation. I stand in a chain of Jews who cared for each other, especially for the less-fortunate, and as a result pioneered innovative structures of social welfare that the world now takes for granted. My heritage teaches me to endure through oppression, persecution, and difficulty, to remain loyal under all circumstances to foundational principles, and, whenever possible, to contribute notable advances for the welfare, not only of Jews, but of all peoples. To stand in this chain of tradition fills me with enormous pride, but also with determination that the heritage will continue.

I stand before the specific Jewish community that I serve. Rabbi Israel Salanter (founder of the *Musar* (Ethical) movement in the middle of the eighteenth century in Poland) spoke to the role of the rabbi. He said: "If a man is truly a rabbi, he will always challenge enough of the congregation that they will want to chase him out of town. But if he is also a *mensch*, they will never do so." To be the leader in a glass house whose job sometimes involves throwing stones is a perilous balancing act, but that is what it means to be a rabbi. It requires respect for where the congregation and community are, but also vision for where they ought to be going. It involves sensing the heart of each individual Jew, comforting and discomforting, pushing, prodding, pulling but always loving. I am the first to confess that I have not always been equal to this high mandate, but knowing that I stand before my Jewish community gives me a goal exalted enough to respect even when its standards exceed my capabilities.

Finally, I stand before myself. It should be self-evident for anyone, and certainly for a rabbi, but one of the dominating words in any vocabulary ought to be "integrity." It is in mine. There must be a substantial correspondence between the words of my mouth and the inner meditations of my heart (Ps 19:15). Sometimes a public figure is called on to say things about which he or she has personal reservations. It comes with the role. But even then, I have striven to come to a private understanding of personally troubling language that would permit me to read the words with multiple levels of comprehension. A good example of this personal clarification is my article entitled "With A Clear Prayer We Could See Forever" (*The Reform Jewish Quarterly* (Fall 2010) 116–37) in which I tried to work through the meaning of the idea of "salvation" as it appears in Reform Jewish liturgy.

There is an old Jewish joke. "How does a Jew answer a question?" "With another question." Centuries of Talmudic give-and-take have taught us that the question is often more important than the answer. Questions frame the debate and direct the conversation. This book is far more about questions than answers, especially definitive answers. It's about how a liberal person who is committed to a religious perspective might go about searching through historic tradition and contemporary experience to process troublesome issues and to approach soul-satisfying answers to some very basic questions. It does not pretend to provide the once-and-forever solution to these quandaries. I have too much respect for the variety of individual inclinations to think that everyone will ever agree. But it does represent my own struggles to come to terms with these issues, and that, at least, is a start.

So now I stand before you, readers, openly to share my ideas about twelve themes that have at times been troublesome tribulations, but which have consistently formed the core of over five decades of rabbinical striving and service.

Beyond the personal ambition to make sense of the road I have traveled, I also humbly hope that my modest efforts might inspire others to engage in thoughtful self-scrutiny regarding their own religious convictions. The future of religion (and certainly of Judaism) depends, I believe, on a heightened understanding and self-consciousness of what we profess.

So now to the twelve essays that deal with the people and the issues that have been the focus of my career.

1

A Sacred Partnership: Covenant

SOCRATES IS REPUTED TO have said that an unexamined life is not worth living. So let our self-examination begin with two very basic questions. Why am I a Jew? And why have I devoted the largest part of my waking hours over the past five-plus decades to Jewish activity?

For many people, perhaps most Jewish lay people, partial answers suffice. "I am Jewish because my family was Jewish." "I am Jewish because the memory of the Holocaust compels me to be so." "I am Jewish because of my connection with Israel." Or to Jewish history or to Jewish rituals (especially the Passover *seder*) or to Judaism's fearless tradition of intellectual inquiry or because some special individual inspired me.

None of these answers is in any way bad or wrong. They are simply inadequate for a person who dedicates his or her career to an encompassing Jewish commitment. There has to be more; there has to be some comprehensive and overarching rationale that makes sense of the entire enterprise, both personally and professionally.

For me, as for a multitude of others, that which accords purpose and meaning is the conviction that I am personally linked in covenant with God, with the Supreme Power of the Universe. Having said that, however, it is important to examine what we might mean by "covenant." There are, after all, different kinds of covenants.

One species of covenant is unilateral. It is imposed by one party on the other who does not have the option of accepting or agreeing, but only to be bound by the terms of the new arrangement. Thus, the Versailles Treaty that marked the formal end of WWI was dictated by the victorious Allied Powers and enforced upon Germany with only the latter's grudging submission. The covenant of Sinai described in chapters 19-20 of the book of Exodus appears as such a one-sided covenant. In that account, Moses ascends the mountain amid awesome and terrifying natural phenomena, and God informs him of the terms of the new relationship. It does not matter that God promises the Israelites that they shall be a kingdom of priests and a holy nation, that God would be their God and that they would have a special relationship with the deity (Exod 19:5-6). The reality is that this covenant was entirely God's doing, and the Israelites were never asked their opinion.

This kind of unilateral covenant may be imposed because one party is vastly more powerful than the other or because there is simply no alternative to acceptance. A midrash tells us that, when God wanted the Israelites to accept his covenant and the Torah that embodied its provisions, Mount Sinai was suspended over their heads. "If you accept the Torah," God allegedly exclaimed, "all will be well. If not, I shall drop the mountain on you" (b. Shabbat 88a).

I may be presumptuous and overly self-impressed, but I maintain enough self-respect and autonomy to believe that any covenant worthy of my adherence cannot be unilateral. Apparently, this was also the attitude of many of our forebears. In Exodus 24:9-11, Moses and the elders visit God again at the summit of Sinai, this despite earlier warnings that Moses alone was allowed to ascend and that all the others, including cattle, should distance themselves from the mountain. In this version of the encounter, the leadership cadre responds by saying "All that the Lord has said, we shall heed and we shall do." To be sure, even this covenant is not between equal parties; God and human beings are not adjudged as peers. Yet the human role in forging the fundamental terms that would govern the relationship is manifest and inescapable. We are reminded of another often-cited midrash in which God shuttles among the tribes of the ancient Middle East, seeking a people that would accept and act on the Torah. Each group in its turn demurs, bringing forward reasons why it would be inappropriate for them to become God's Torah partner. Only when God offers the Torah to the Israelites do we find a wholehearted acceptance that they could be in covenant with God as the bearers of Torah in the world. Despite the patently self-congratulatory tone of this early legend, the aspect of covenantal mutuality is obvious.

Unilateral–mutual is not the only dichotomy when it comes to a consideration of covenant. For the prophets who spoke in the name of God before the Babylonian Exile (prior to 587 BCE), the covenant was largely a collective agreement, and individuals participated in it only by virtue of their belonging to the group. By the time the Jews returned from the Exile (538 BCE), Jeremiah had elaborated a new concept of covenant that inhered in the individual human heart (Jer 31:31-34). Ezekiel made it abundantly clear (especially in chapter 18) that God's consideration began with each single person. While some attention to the relationship of God and the Israelite nation persisted through succeeding millennia, it has been the revolutionary change from the sixth century BCE that has characterized Jewish life ever since. In subsequent centuries, it has influenced the development of Christianity and other world religions and even constitutes one of the basic pillars of modern individualism. It forms a critical and central element of my own Jewish identity.

Integral to the notion of covenantal individuality is the idea of perpetuality. The collective covenant of the pre-Exilic prophets could be ruptured by widespread deviation from covenantal expectations. Amos, Hosea, Micah, and 1 Isaiah understood the impending Assyrian assault and the subsequent Babylonian Exile as God's punishment of the people for their violations of the collective covenant and, in fact, as the severing of that relationship. Yet even the pre-Exilic author of Deuteronomy insisted that the covenant between God and the Jews was eternal. He wrote: "Neither with you only do I make this covenant and this oath; but with them who are not here with us this day" (29:13-14). The covenant of which the Deuteronomist wrote was to carry forward through the generations, to be everlasting, an idea that makes it possible for me to place myself directly in a continuum that reaches back in unbroken fashion to our earliest antecedents. That reality gives meaning and purpose to my life and fills me with a feeling of being remarkably special.

One of the most powerful ways I have thought about "covenant" has to do with the question of whether the revelation at Sinai included specific content or not. The report of the event in the book of Exodus makes it very clear that the biblical editors believed that specific words had been conveyed from God to Moses. These words are recorded, they would have us believe, in the Torah. From a traditional perspective, every word of the first five books of the Hebrew Scriptures is the exact transcript of what God commanded Moses to write down and teach the newly freed Israelites. But tradition goes further. The Pharisees, perhaps a thousand or more years later than the revelation at Sinai, and their rabbinic successors, posited that a second Torah, the Oral Torah, had also been disclosed to Moses. The

Oral Torah contained all correct understandings, interpretations and applications of the Written Torah. Since these extensions of the Law derived directly from the God-spoken Written Law, they were equally invested with divine authority and were declared to be as binding as the words spoken at Sinai. The Oral Law is codified in the *Babylonian Talmud*, which, together with its own commentaries and interpretations remains the unalterable basis for Orthodox Judaism to this day.

Biblical scholarship since the nineteenth century has challenged the idea that every word in the text we possess today derives from Sinai. Beginning in Germany and now throughout the scholarly world, researchers identify elements of the present Torah text as originating in different environments and at different times. Some material is relatively early, deriving from the period of the divided kingdoms of Israel and Judea, carried forward separately for several centuries and identified by their characteristic use of reference to God by either the name Yahweh (the "J" code) or Elohim (the "E" code). Somewhat later (scholars propose that it was before the year 621 BCE) another corpus of text emerged. This material, which forms the basis for the book of Deuteronomy, represents a reality after the destruction of the northern ten tribes of Israel at the hands of the Assyrians in 722-721 and before the exile of the Judeans by the Babylonians in 587. During this century and a third, the priesthood of Jerusalem successfully asserted a monopoly over cultic worship and demanded that three times each year people appear with tribute sacrifices at "the place where God has proclaimed His name," the Temple in Jerusalem. All competitive tribal sanctuaries had been eliminated by the Assyrians (except for the insignificant alternative of Benjamin that was easily bypassed by the Jerusalemites). The centricity of Jerusalem is a major element of the "D" code, but that document also includes a structure in which good deeds are invariably rewarded and evil actions punished. Even later, possibly following the return from the Babylonian Exile in 538, priestly editors created yet more material that enshrined their particular interests and that we now find in Leviticus and much of the later chapters of Exodus and some of Numbers (the "P" code). Finally, likely some time between 500 and 450 BCE, the priests consolidated all this (and possibly other fragments of text) into a single, authoritative document that would serve as the basic constitutional law of the Second Commonwealth. This canonized text is the Torah we now possess, virtually unaltered for the past 2,500 years.

When one reads the Torah (or any other document), it is important to identify one's *a priori* assumptions about the text. If, for example, the reader begins with the conviction that every word we have in the Torah today, even every letter, was spoken by God at Sinai, then there are ways to harmonize and rationalize what might otherwise appear to be inconsistencies and conflicts within the text. If, on the other hand, the beginning assumption is that one will read the text as a piece of literature, however religious and inspirational in nature, and let the text speak for itself, then an altogether different picture emerges. The latter reader comes away with the conclusion that the Torah we have today bears the unmistakable imprint of human agency. There is no methodology of which I am aware that can conclusively segregate those words that God said to Moses from words later authored by prophets and priests.

The problem of this scholarly approach with regard to covenant is "How can you base any kind of enduring covenant between God and the Jew (or the Jewish people) when you cannot know what the real terms of the revelation are?" One answer is to say that we ought simply to affirm the Torah as we have it today, as our predecessors did over the centuries, and ignore questions of authorship and authority. A second response might be that there are certain elements of the Torah (and the Bible in general) that have become so widely accepted that they can be regarded as God's words. Thus, the Ten Commandments are often accorded special status. The Classical Reform Judaism in which I was raised styled itself as "Prophetic Judaism," giving priority to the ethical pronouncements of the Torah and the prophets and denigrating the cultic and ritual material we attribute to the priests. Again, it's a matter of how you begin, what *a priori* assumptions you adopt at the outset of the inquiry.

I have come to another perspective that depends on the insights of a great German-Jewish philosopher, Martin Buber. In 1935 as Nazi laws increased pressure on Germany's Jews, Buber moved from Berlin to Jerusalem, where he remained for the rest of his life, teaching at the Hebrew University. In 1923, however, Buber had written a remarkable small book, *Ich und Du*, translated into English in 1937 as *I and Thou*. I was first exposed to this book as a junior in college, and I frankly admit I really had no clue as to what Buber was saying. Yes, I understood intellectually that he had analyzed human relationships into two categories. Most of our contacts with other people, he wrote, are distant and instrumental; we do not think of the other person as a real human being, but as a device for accomplishing some task. Thus, the clerk at the convenience store is not someone who has a family, who has cares and joys, who struggles to pay bills on a minimum-wage salary and about whom we are concerned, but as an extension of the cash register whose function is to scan our purchase and give us the right change . . . "Have a nice day!" But there are also occasional relationships of intense intimacy. These Buber characterized as I-Thou, using the German pronoun "du" which at the time that he was writing was employed only for special relationships, such as spouse-to-spouse, parent-to-child, and very close and long-time friends. I-Thou relationships are characterized by nonverbal communication and understanding, the ability of a partner to know what the other person is thinking without words, the ability ac-curately to finish the other person's sentence, the intuitive insight to know what gifts and words will be appreciated and what will not be accepted gracefully. It requires a certain amount of life experience and maturity fully to comprehend this binary analysis of relationships, and that probably did not completely come to me until I was in my forties.

When I finally understood what Buber was driving at, however, a corollary emerged. Toward the end of this dense and difficult book, Buber shifts from the individual to a consideration of the collective, of the ap-plication of his idea to the relationship of God to the entire people of Israel gathered at Sinai. What he suggests is that what occurred at Sinai was not the revelation of specific content, but the creation of a collective I-Thou relationship of covenant. From that moment on, it became the central task of the individual Jew and the collective Jewish people to puzzle out the specific terms of the covenant. "What," they had to ask themselves, "given our particular circumstances does it mean to live in covenant with God? How should we conduct ourselves to be worthy of this relationship with the most sacred Holy One?" The distillate of their inquiries is recorded as the Torah, representing some eight hundred years of spiritual search from Sinai until canonization. But the search does not end in 450 BCE. Circumstances and conditions change. A person living in the technological twenty-first century is obviously subject to different influences and needs compared to a biblical shepherd at a Judean oasis; a shtetl Jew in a Ukrainian village of the late nineteenth century, surrounded by hostile non-Jews and subsisting at the bare margins of survival is obviously a very different person than a middle-class Jew in a free and accepting American ambience.

The struggle for me—and for others like me—is first to appreciate these differences and what they might imply for the received texts and wisdom of the past and then to pose and answer for myself the identical questions raised by Buber but asked ever since Sinai. Because this endeavor places the individual at the center of the spiritual quest, I have come to think of the position that is most comfortable for me as "religious humanism." As something of an historian, I rejoice that this epithet links me to the great religious humanists of the Renaissance, such as Reuchlin and Erasmus, Pico della Mirandola and Machiavelli and Thomas More. Theirs is a heritage of spiritual search worth treasuring and emulating. And I rejoice that the concept of religious humanism enables me to think of myself as a potentially worthy covenant partner with the God who was first manifest to my ancestors at Sinai, but who can equally be apparent to me in today's modern life. I believe that this stance exalts the human being without in any way diminishing the divine reality.

Over the years, Jews have been oppressed and persecuted because they claimed (or it was claimed about them) that they were "the chosen people." At times, we have shifted the responsibility from God to ourselves, asserting that we are "the choosing people." It is without embarrassment that I express my pride and pleasure at having a special relationship with God and with the people who saw themselves as belonging to a perpetual covenant with the Eternal Power of the Universe.

I can make this unadulterated assertion because I do not believe that God has only one covenant with human beings. To say that the covenant is exclusive to one group is by extension to impose a limitation on God. But, as I shall assert in a later chapter, if God is infinite, then the idea of human beings restricting that infinitude is an impossibility.

Over the years, I have come to believe that people are divided into two types. There are "monists" who claim that they are in possession of the truth/the way/the covenant and that all others are wrong, sinful, damned. There are, of course, religious communions that take this position and assert that "salvation is of the Lord," provided that the Lord is the deity only as they understand Him. The alternative to monism is "pluralism," which in religious terms means that there are many ways to live a good and godly life. In the New Testament, there appears to be an ambiguous attitude toward this dichotomy. In the one hand, Matthew talks of fulfilling the Law, but John speaks of abrogating it in favor of a new covenant. This same gospel (John 14:5-6) states emphatically that there is only one way to reach God, whereas the Epistle to the Romans (11:28-29) asserts that the covenant of Sinai is irrevocable. This may reflect that Matthew and Romans represent a generation of Christian hope that Jews would join the new religion, while John, written perhaps thirty years later, evinces frustration and anger that they have refused. Which is the right path? Consider the following analogy.

Suppose you want to travel from my hometown, Corpus Christi, TX to our state capitol, Austin. Most people would say that you should hop in the car, zoom up I-37, circumnavigate San Antonio on I-410 and then take I-35 to Austin. But clearly this is not the only way to complete the trip. You could fly, connecting in either Houston or Dallas, or charter a private plane. You could drive a variety of indirect, rural routes . . . or ride a bicycle . . . or a horse . . . or hike . . . or skateboard . . . or . . . The point is obvious: you can achieve the same goal in a wide variety of ways. So what is the right way? The one that satisfies your style and spiritual quest. If you have a noon meeting in Austin but want to be home for dinner, interstate highway travel might be most suitable. On the other hand, if you want to see spring wildflowers, air travel at 30,000 feet or racing along the highway at 75 mph will likely be frustrating.

If we substitute a spiritual goal for Austin, the same lesson applies. It is incumbent upon each individual to assess his or her own needs and desires and then to find a religious path that satisfies those criteria. An infinite God makes possible an array of covenantal relationships, and no one who seeks a legitimate spiritual connection with the divine need feel excluded. This is the essence of pluralism, and it is decidedly my perspective. Besides, as a Jew and a member of a minority religious group, if monism were to prevail, there would certainly be no place for us; we would always be outvoted, diminished, excluded, and even annihilated. Jewish survival is only possible in a society that encourages pluralism.

The covenant to which I voluntarily subscribe is necessarily mutual. Its obligations and responsibilities emanate from its reciprocal nature. God provides a special relationship to the Jewish people, and the people, in return, agree to live by the dictates of what they understand to be God's will. But in a theological system, such as the one to which I have given my allegiance and which is grounded substantially in the teachings of Martin Buber, the covenant is a relationship not based on a specific revelation of content. Rather, to use a frequent analogy, it is like the speechless closeness of a long-married couple for whom presence is more important than words. Without specific language, there is still security and trust, faith, inspiration, motivation, and purpose; there is a sense of confidence that surpasses any verbiage.

From where, then, do the detailed terms of such a covenant emerge? From the determination of the individual in covenant with God to live a life worthy of this relationship. It has been roughly 3350 years since that original meeting at the top of Sinai. Ever since that time, Jews have striven to understand what the ethical and moral ramifications of a life of covenant ought to be. The distillate of those efforts is presented to us in the form of a variety of classic, historical documents that collectively represent the accumulated answers to the challenge of covenant—but each a human response, certainly inspired by God, but created at a particular time and influenced by specific social, political and other circumstances. In each generation, Jews strove to know what they should do to be worthy of being in covenant with God. How they should live at the highest standard of human existence in order to repair a broken world and in order to bring into existence in human society the values they understood to be endorsed by God. The specific rituals each generation carried forward and new ones they created served to express in concrete terms the abstract values embodied in the covenant. As the conditions of Jewish life changed, their answers to the question of how to live in consonance with the covenant also changed so as better to pursue the larger goal in the developing context of their daily lives. To be sure, each generation based a good part of its contemporary answers on the collected wisdom of past Jewish ages. But no Jewish generation has ever shied away from an attempt to bring the age-old values and wisdom into correspondence with the realities of their current situation. During most of the rabbinic period, the traditional halachic authorities were noted for their ability to be flexible in the face of changing circumstances, and even when the Hatam Sofer (Moses Schreiber, 1762-1839) famously declared that what is new is forbidden by the Torah (*Hadash asur min haTorah*), other equally Orthodox authorities were demonstrating that innovation and flexibility were still possible within a traditional context. Reform Judaism, to which I have wholeheartedly given my assent, has championed the process of continual updating and readjustment since its inception in the early nineteenth century. We clearly live with one foot securely anchored in the wisdom of the past, but equally we are firmly connected to the needs and issues of the present and to creative ways through which we might address them. This ongoing dynamic persists as we search out ways to be faithful to the covenant that has characterized our people since Sinai.

There are corollary consequences to the notion of a mutual covenant that may shock and dismay some people, even as they enthuse me. Those corollaries have to do with the nature of God. The Bible speaks a good deal about attributes of God (see, for example, Exod 34:6-7) and even more about divine actions. But the tradition is relatively silent regarding the essential nature of God, except in relatively discrete eras, such as the time of Maimonides who, in his *Moreh Nevukhim*, dealt extensively with the subject of God's essence and attributes. God is, for example, simply presumed to exist prior to the creation described in the first chapter of Genesis. And yet to assert that the Israelites (and their later Jewish successors) had a covenant with God suggests two surprising, but logical, conclusions regarding the divine nature.

If one inquires about the essence of covenant in general, the common element is that each of the parties possesses something the others want and that they are willing to engage in a trading process to fulfill their individual needs. Thus, if one goes to an automobile dealership, the dealer has cars but wants the customer's money, while the customer has money (cash, loans, trade-in) but needs the dealer's car. They are prepared to enter into a covenant (sales agreement) in which each party contributes his or her own possession in exchange for receiving an item or service from the other.

Inherent in this swap is a faith or trust that each party places in the partner. An auto dealer would not sell a car to someone who was likely to abscond or default on the payments, nor would the purchaser enter into an agreement unless there was a basic trust that the dealer would deliver the promised vehicle free of defects. In religious terms, there should be no surprise or shock that Jews should trust God and have faith that God will fulfill his side of the bargain. What is worth noting, however, is the faith and trust in humanity and in the Jewish people implied by a covenantal relationship. When God entered into covenant with the former slaves at Sinai and when God continues that covenant through the ages, it is as if God is saying: "I have faith in this people that they are determined and able enough to bring My principles and values into reality in the world." That God trusts and values us as partners is the first of two remarkable corollaries to the existence of the covenant. I cannot imagine a statement that more empowers human beings and that, at the same time, places a greater burden of responsibility on them to live up to the challenge. It is exhilarating, exalting and exhausting, all at the same time.

Now to the second corollary consequence of a mutual covenant as it relates to the nature of God. The essence of a covenant is that both parties have needs. But if God has needs, then God cannot be complete or perfect.

In the next chapter, when I write about "God and Prayer," I shall take the position that the only attribute of the Eternal that I find non-debatable is that God is infinite. Accepting the consequence of mutuality, however, on the surface sounds like something of a contradiction to the notion of divine infinitude. How can something be both infinite and incomplete at the same time? Can an infinite God also change and develop; is novelty inconsistent with infinitude?

At first blush one might surmise (as I did) that this poses a dilemma. And I candidly admit that I do not have a complete resolution to the problem, even though I have found a few ways to assuage my uncertainty, if not to set the matter completely at rest.

The first idea that makes some sense to me is that the fourfold definition of God that most of us were taught in beginning classes on the philosophy of religion is neither biblical nor Jewish, but, in fact, the product of the Christian Middle Ages. We all learned that God is omnipresent, omniscient, omnipotent, and benevolent. But that's classic Thomas Aquinas speaking, not the book of Genesis. In one of my favorite episodes of all Scripture (chapter 18), Abraham and God stand together on a hill overlooking the evil cities of Sodom and Gomorrah. God proposes to destroy Sodom, but apparently God has imperfect knowledge of what is transpiring there. In verse 21, God says: "Let Me go down and determine whether they are wreaking havoc in equal measure to the shrieking that is coming to Me. If not, I will know." The God of Abraham is a God of limited knowledge, hardly omniscient. Otherwise, the investigative expedition makes little sense. Only a few verses later (25), Abraham has to remind God of a core ethical principle of the divine teaching. The patriarch speaks almost impudently to God and says: "Far be it from You to do such a thing, killing innocent and wicked alike, so that the innocent and the wicked suffer the same fate. Far be it from You! Must not the Judge of all the earth do justly?" I fully understand that this question can be seen as simply a rhetorical device in which Abraham challenged God to remember and to live up to his principles. We don't know the source of these principles, but, apparently, they were conventional wisdom because God immediately admits that He has to rethink the destructive intent. If God hasn't considered the consequences of divine utterances and threats, does this not suggest that God's knowledge is incomplete? Other questions voiced by God, such as those posed to Adam and Eve in Genesis 3:9 and 3:11 and to Cain in Genesis 4:9 are more likely rhetorical, but still might betray a suspicion of divine ignorance. If one follows the premise of William of Occam, might this not be the simplest and, therefore, preferred reading of the text? After all, the gods of the peoples among whom the ancient Israelites lived were hardly omniscient. Why should we believe that their Israelite equivalent had to be?

So the biblical and Jewish record, at least up to the age of Maimonides (twelfth century) and even thereafter seems comfortable with the notion of a God who is fallible and incomplete. That prospect does not dismay me. Over the years I have found that it is very difficult for me to establish and sustain a relationship with a person who is categorically different from myself. We use the phrase "holier than thou" as a put-off; we distance ourselves intuitively from people who do not share basic elements of our humanness. If God exhibits some of the qualities that I find in myself and in other people, this makes it much more possible for me to have an ongoing, intimate relationship with the Divine.

A second way I have found to handle this apparent dilemma is through radical agnosticism. Like biblical Job, I am quite prepared to admit and accept that there are things I simply cannot fathom. If I am finite (as contrasted to God's infinitude), then my ability to know and comprehend must be limited. In short, I affirm my status as a human being. There is so much more about people and the world around us that I do not know (but could), that it causes me no discomfort to admit that there may be secrets of the universe that are beyond me. After all, if I am prepared to question God's omniscience, far be it for me then to assert my own!

The third way in which I have tried to come to grips with the seeming disparity between God's infinitude and God's needfulness and incompleteness is by positing that inherent in the concept of divine infinitude is the potential for infinite growth, development and change. If this appears as something of a contradiction, then I ask myself to consider whether infinite and complete are really synonyms or whether they are two different categories of the divine nature.

As in so many areas of life, I am prepared to live with a measure of uncertainty in theology. I am committed to the existence of a covenant between God and me, individually and as a member of the Jewish people. *Dayyenu*, that ought to be enough.

2

Let Me Speak to You: God and Prayer

THE HOLOCAUST HAS BEEN the most transformative influence in regard to Jewish thinking about God and prayer, at least since the destruction of the Second Temple in Jerusalem by the Roman army in 70 CE At the time of that ancient cataclysm, Jewish ritual practice was completely reconstituted; the biblical model of a sacrificial cult located in a central sanctuary was replaced by a rabbinic scheme focusing on prayer in the home and in the synagogue. Yet there is no indication that the rabbis rejected the biblical notion of God. At the same time that nascent Christianity was accommodating to Graeco-Roman Neoplatonic ideas of a distant and unmoving deity and an intermediate active intellect (logos), the center of Jewish civilization shifted from the destroyed Jerusalem to the Galilee and then to the Mesopotamian valleys where Greek philosophy and religion exercised far less impact than in the regions where Christianity was developing. As a result, there was only minimal pressure to abandon the biblical notion of a proximate and active God in normative rabbinic circles.

The universal impact of the Shoah, however, has dictated a far-reaching re-evaluation of Jewish religious belief. Even for someone like myself who suffered no personal or familial loss during the Nazi era, the tragedy of WWII's "war against the Jews" has created a massive and unavoidable challenge to traditional belief.

In the Hebrew Bible, God is depicted as intimately and actively interacting with human beings. One of my favorite chapters of the Torah is Genesis 18 in which God and Abraham stand together, much like friends, and converse about the fate of Sodom and Gomorrah. This is no Neoplatonic God who, as the unmoving source of all other motion, cannot even react to prayer. This is a God who is "near to all who call upon Him" (Ps 145:18), who creates and destroys, who speaks and who acts, who listens and responds; this is a God who is intimately involved with the physical universe and with all that is therein.

The omnipotent God of the biblical creation and of Aquinas is only one perception of God in Scripture. In Exodus, God is manifest as a henotheistic deity, residing exclusively in a series of particular locales. Thus, Moses must leave Egypt to be in God's presence at the burning bush, and later (Exod 24) we read of God holding court and entertaining the Israelite leadership at the top of Mount Sinai. Especially in Deuteronomy, God's home is in the Temple in Jerusalem, "the place where He has proclaimed His name." The book of Jonah is, in part, a polemic against this notion of a geographically limited God; that Jonah believes he can flee from God makes no sense unless he also believes that God cannot transcend the boundaries of Judea—and of course he is proved wrong about this assumption. The omnipresent, universal God of the Second Isaiah is only a late development in the biblical scheme of God images. The later rabbis developed the notion of the *Shekhinah*, a female image through which God can become immanently manifest, especially as an indwelling, caring and ubiquitous presence. There is a Hasidic idea that God resides wherever we let God in. But in all post-exilic Jewish religion, the universalistic concept of Isaiah is the one concept that triumphs over the other more restricted ideas.

The Holocaust makes it very difficult, if not impossible, to sustain this traditional concept of a God who beneficently and potently intervenes in human affairs. The issue is often summarized by the question "Where was God at Auschwitz?" In a more complete formulation, the challenge to traditional theism is expressed thus: If God is a God who intervenes in human affairs, could there have been a more apt time for such an intrusion than during the horrific murder of eleven million people in the Nazi death camps and killing fields? Would one not have expected an interventional God of merciful and beneficent character to have halted the slaughter of one and a half million Jewish children? These are questions that ought to threaten traditional theistic belief for all religious people, but they are more poignant and immediate for Jews because, after all, these were our relatives and these were our own children. The challenge is inescapable and wrenching.

The problem of theodicy (the apparent miscarriage of divine justice and the persistence of evil) is the most enduring and perplexing concern for anyone who strives to maintain a belief in God. Job resolved the issue by asserting that a divine master plan existed, but that he, fallible human that he was, could not know it. Such radical agnosticism may be sufficient for some believers. Deists have held to the notion of *Deus Absconditus*, of a creator God who was involved at the beginning, but who then left the terrestrial scene to the uninterrupted devices of the human species. From the biblical concept of henotheism to various iterations of modern religious thought, there have been proposals of a limited God who either cannot intervene or who chooses not to limit the unfettered range of human free will.

I want to add a comment about "the unfettered range of human free will." There are some who would argue that this phrase is a redundancy. If human will is free, then it is by definition unfettered; free is free. I take a slightly different posture. Divine freedom may be absolute, but human free will is not. Its scope is limited by a variety of factors. First among these limitations is biology. Our possibilities are restricted by our race, our gender, our innate intelligence, our size and strength—by many given factors. We are further constrained by our family of origin and the choices they made and the legacy, financial, spiritual, and intellectual, they bequeathed to us. And the values to which we have committed ourselves form boundaries around our human freedom. In short, while divine freedom may be unlimited, human freedom of will and action is unfettered, but only within the bounds of our human potentials and restraints. Among the more interesting of these modern proponents of a non-absolute deity have been Alfred North Whitehead and Charles Hartshorne who proposed in their idea of "process theology" that God will be forever incomplete and that God grows and develops to incorporate novelty, much as human beings change to adapt to new circumstances.

Every one of these proposals for the solution of the problem of theodicy has something to recommend it, but each of them also entails shortcomings and, in my view, falls short of satisfaction. There is no completely adequate answer to this challenge, and that is why it persists as a troublesome and vexing tribulation.

The crux of the issue for someone like myself who has taught the Jewish religion in classrooms and from the pulpit for multiple decades is: "How does one stand before the people of Israel who have been so ravaged by the horrors of the Holocaust and still speak of God, even use the word 'God" with integrity? Can I say the words that are required of me as a rabbi with, at minimum, a personal sense of honesty? Can I simultaneously stand before the historical tradition that I am pledged to represent, before the contemporary survivors of the most terrifying evil that human beings could ever imagine and, ultimately, before myself and do what I am called to do with self-respect?"

The late German-Canadian Jewish philosopher Emil Fackenheim frequently spoke of the 614th commandment: "Thou shalt not hand Hitler posthumous victories. To despair of the God of Israel is to confirm Hitler's work for him." I suspect, then, that it is not accidental that my all-time favorite congregational name is of a liberal synagogue, founded by German refugees in the suburbs of Buenos Aires, Argentina. Its founders chose the Hebrew name *Lamrot Hakol*, "In Spite of Everything," for their congregation. In spite of every assault on Jewish survival over the last three thousand years, we have persisted. It is not uncommon for us to remind ourselves—and the world—that those who persecuted us and tried to destroy us have largely perished, while we have survived, beaten down, but unbowed. After the Holocaust to demonstrate their determination and persistence, some Jews named their daughters *Nili*, which is an acronym of part of the verse *Netzach Yisrael Lo Yeshakair*, "The Victorious One of Israel will not be belied" (1 Sam 15:29).

Yet persistence alone is insufficient. In its early days, the new state of Israel offered the rationale "Never Again." And at the outset that was enough justification for Israel and its worldwide Zionist supporters. But as the years have passed, it has become obvious that one cannot build a positive identity on a negation. One must elaborate what one stands *for* and not simply what one stands *against*. The same principle holds true in theology. That the traditional concept of God no longer functions effectively, particularly in the light of the Holocaust, may be true, but that realization does not provide adequate positive rationale for a continuing belief in God. It is incumbent upon those of us who would speak of God and who would hope to make God a living reality for our people to adumbrate a positive idea of deity that can be accepted with integrity in the twenty-first century.

I can only speak for myself, but I have found a way to think and talk about God that works for me. I call this concept "perceptual theology." It proceeds from the dogmatic statement that God is infinite, while in every respect created entities are finite. As a human being, I recognize that my size is limited, my intelligence is limited, my resources and wealth are limited, as are my goodness and even my life span. Judaism also posits that the divine infinitude is unitary, so that in the oneness of God all potential attributes of God may be apprehended. The corollary of these propositions is nearly panentheistic, namely, that every characteristic of God that a human may perceive is already in God. A second corollary is that a finite entity can never perceive the entirety of an infinite entity, but only some part or aspect of it at any given time. Consider this analogy. If a person looks at a closed book, he or she may easily describe the size of the book, the colors of the cover, the design, etc. But the observer cannot make any statements about the inside of the volume. However, if the book is now opened, the person can make a fairly good description of the interior but has lost the ability to visualize (and thus describe) the outside. Perception depends on the relationship of the viewer and the object to be viewed. And if this is true with regard to a small and finite object, like a book, then how much more true must it be with regard to perception of an infinite object, God. A human being's ability to perceive some aspect of God depends, therefore, on the stance in relationship to God that the person adopts. This stance is not physical but psychological. So, for example, if I am standing at the newborn nursery in a maternity hospital, I might become aware of God as Creator of miracles. I might realize that there are billions of cells that flush through a fetus during gestation and that deficiencies in the DNA and chromosomes of even a tiny fraction of these cells might lead to a birth defect. Yet, here before me are infants, all different to be sure, but all relatively healthy and with the requisite equipment in the right place and functioning more-or-less properly. To my mind, this is little short of a divine miracle, given the immense odds that something could have gone wrong during pregnancy. On the other hand, if I leave the hospital and walk out into a beautiful spring day, I am likely to notice that nature is being reborn in myriad ways, grass and budding flowers and warmth of air, and that birds are migrating on accustomed flyways to ancestral summer homes. My perception of God will then shift from Creator of miracles to Sustainer of the natural order. When I drive out of the parking lot, I might be confronted by a wholly different situation as a large truck weaves out of its lane and rushes straight at my car. No more am I thinking of God in naturalistic terms; now, the God of whom I am aware is a Savior and Rescuer, whose immediate intervention and help I solicit with heartfelt plea to avoid an accident. In all of these cases, God has not changed, because the infinitude of God contains all of these attributes, as well as any others that I could imagine. What has altered is my relationship to God; I am perceiving different aspects of divinity because I am in a different psychological relationship to God. (I acknowledge my intellectual debt in this theory to the study of both epistemology and phenomenology and, in some respects, to the idea of "deconstructionism" that emerged from the thought of Jacques Derrida in the 1960s.)

Are there aspects or attributes of God with which I have never had any relationship? Unquestionably! But this cannot mean that these attributes do not exist. On the contrary, it can only mean that I have never been in the stance that would make it possible for me to perceive that characteristic. The responsibility is not God's, nor does this in any way indicate that such a perception is impossible. That I have not, for example, had a personal, mutual dialogue with God, as Abraham had on the hillside over Sodom and Gomorrah, does not mean that this could not happen tomorrow; it simply suggests that I have not placed myself in the right relationship to the infinite Godhead or opened myself sufficiently to take advantage of this aspect of God's infinite potential. The burden of experiencing the sacred has shifted from God's self-revelation to man's discovery. To say that such a conversation can never occur is to allege that there is a limitation in God's potential, and this would violate the axiom with which I began this analysis.

This notion of "perceptual theology" has clear implications for the nature of prayer. I understand all prayer as conversation, but conversation with any one or more of four partners. The classical way of thinking about prayer is, obviously, that it is a conversation directed toward God. It is a subsidiary question whether God in any way responds to that prayer; what is critical is the intention of the person who prays. In this regard, it makes a great deal of difference what attribute of the infinite God one is addressing. If, for example, I am responding to a perception of God as Creator of the miraculous, I might utter a prayer of thanksgiving. But I am unlikely to anticipate a divine response to this utterance. So, too, if the aspect of God to which I am drawn is that which sustains order in the natural world, my prayer of praise will hardly elicit a divine response. I would not expect the impersonal and abstract power of the universe to communicate with me in the manner of another personality. That would constitute an illogical expectation, an anticipation that doesn't make sense. On the other hand, I might listen more carefully for a response if my prayer is one of petition and the attribute of God with which I am in contact is one of a personal nature.

There is another prayer-partner to whom I might address my words. This is my neighbor, perhaps the person sitting near me in the synagogue sanctuary. Let me offer two examples. First, consider the prayer known as the *mi shebeirach*, the prayer most often recited during the time that the Torah lies on the reading desk. Before the prayer itself is sung, worshippers often speak out loud the names of people who are ill and whose welfare and health are of importance to those who voice their names. Aside from the plea to God for healing, we are also offering two bits of information to those around us. First, we are informing them, should they not already know, that a particular individual is in distress. Quite often, I notice from the pulpit that members of the congregation react when some name is spoken: "I did not know so-and-so was ill. Thank you for letting me know. Perhaps I can extend some help or at least a loving presence." But second, the person who speaks the name is also telling his or her neighbors that he or she is concerned, that there is a burden of worry and anxiety that weighs heavily on the heart. A second example concerns the mourners' *Kaddish* which is recited toward the end of virtually every service. It has become customary for mourners to rise when the name of a family member is read before the prayer itself. This, too, is a way of informing others that there is a sadness in their lives, that something is different in the constellation of their family and that they would appreciate a warm and friendly greeting following the services. Prayer can be a conversation with one's neighbors.

One may also speak in a virtual way to the generations of Jews who have preceded us. Many of the prayers we use are centuries old; some date back to biblical times. To speak these prayers offers us a way to commune with Jews of ages past and places far removed from our own. In this quasi-mystical experience, we are enabled to participate in Jewish events long past with personalities we might otherwise only encounter in history books. But this skill at "retrojection" is an inherent element of full Jewish maturity. The *Haggadah* of Passover encourages us to migrate through time and space as "Every Jew is obligated to think of himself or herself as though he or she had been personally redeemed from Egyptian slavery." The prayers of the past may not even contain theological concepts with which we agree today, but their antiquity itself permits us the opportunity to be in touch with our historical heritage in a remarkable manner.

Prayer can also be a conversation with oneself. In one of my favorite prayers, we read the following: ". . . when doubt troubles us, when anxiety makes us tremble, and pain clouds the mind, we look inward for the answer to our prayers . . ."[1] This prayer expresses the perspective that the answers to our petitions are already within us, if only we can tease them out. God, the ambience of the worship service and the congregation function collectively

---

1. Chaim Stern, ed., *Gates of Prayer for Shabbat and Weekdays* (New York: Central Conference of American Rabbis, 1994), 79.

like the psychotherapist who calls upon the worshipper/patient to unlock the hidden recesses of the mind and the spirit and to discover therein previously untapped resources of strength, understanding and perspective. Traditional prayers of praise and/or gratitude are also examples of prayers that may be addressed to oneself. Their purpose is not to evoke a change or a response from God, but to produce a heightened sense of awe and thankfulness in the worshipper himself. In this way we speak to ourselves at times when we pray.

Since theological beliefs and prayer are innately personal matters, what I have written may or may not have any application to anyone beyond myself. Nonetheless, it illustrates the positions to which I have arrived and at which I am spiritually comfortable. If they help others on their religious journeys, so much the better.

3

Who Said That: The Bible and Other Sacred Texts

BIBLE

THERE IS A TENDENCY to think of ancient writings as somewhat primitive, certainly superseded in literary merit by more recent creations. Of course, anyone holding such a point of view needs to account for the great Greek dramatists, like Sophocles and Euripides, and their philosophical confreres, Aristotle, Socrates, and Plato; for Archimedes and Galen; for Romans, like Ovid, Cicero, and Lucretius; for a Chinese scholar named Confucius; and for hundreds of other writers, physicians, and scientists from the pre-Christian centuries whose works remain essential parts of the literary canon today. One would also need to add to this list a number of authors, mostly anonymous, whose words appear in the pages of the Hebrew Scriptures.

It might be argued that these literary giants were the exceptions that prove the rule, that the vast bulk of whatever was produced in the ancient world was so deficient in quality that it never merited critical mention, much less a place on the shelves of the historical library of significant and transformative works. That may well be true, except that it is right to remember that literary genius is a rarity in any age, including our own, and that it is perfectly appropriate to single out these outstanding and exceptional authors in their age, even as Chaucer was in his era, Shakespeare in his, and a select number of writers in our own day.

I have probably read the entire Hebrew Scriptures a dozen times, and I have undoubtedly studied and heard the Torah more than fifty times, in classrooms and from the synagogue pulpit. I come away from this exposure with a tremendous sense of awe, admiration, and humility in the face of the frequent literary brilliance of the text. To be sure, there are long and tedious passages that in no wise enrich my life. The extended priestly detail of the sacrificial cult in Leviticus and the prescriptions for ritual and public health purity that follow have scant appeal to me. Nor do the lengthy accounts of the conquest of Canaan in Joshua or the architectural details of the tabernacle and the temple have any impact on my personal identity or religious conviction.

Yet, just when one is tempted to slam the book shut and declare it to be filled with irrelevant historical trivia, a passage will erupt from the page to stun me into rapt appreciation. Virtually every time I have opened the book, I have found new insights and novel perspectives; the Bible is a constant source of surprise and delight. And reading it in Hebrew does make a difference.

Consider on a simple linguistic level the chiastic structure of Genesis 9:6. In that verse, a sequence of three Hebrew words is carefully arranged so that it can be followed by close variants of the same words but in reverse order (thus A, B, C, then C, B, A). In English, the verse is often translated "Whoever sheds a man's blood, by man shall his blood then be shed." As I sit back in my desk chair and think about these words, I am filled with admiration at skill of this anonymous ancient author who so much enjoyed playing with language that he crafted a sentence so obviously deliberate in its structure that even several thousands of years later his mastery of literary form astounds. This is the creation, not of a primitive, but of an immensely skilled professional wordsmith of the ancient world.

Similarly, I cannot read the book of Amos without marveling at the enormous skill with which this author constructed the first two chapters. Speaking to the assembled leadership of the kingdom of Israel in 750 BCE in the temple at Beth El, the prophet begins by castigating each of four neighboring enemies. Citing first Damascus, then Gaza, then Tyre, and finally Edom, Amos tells the Israelites that their hereditary enemies are doomed. Those who heard him certainly shouted their approval and agreement, but they failed to notice that his selection of targets was remarkable and that he bracketed Israel from northeast to southwest, then from northwest to southeast with a crisscross of targeting hairs aimed precisely at Beth El. Even then, he allows them the illusion of safety by speaking harshly about their southern neighbor, the kingdom of Judah. But, finally, when their defenses are down, he hones in on the sin of the Israelites and declares that their sins will be punished with a special ferocity because "You only have I known of all the families of the earth; therefore, I will visit upon you all your iniquities" (3:2). The audacious author of this jeremiad (certainly not Amos himself, since he declares that he is nothing but an itinerant tree trimmer) shows himself to be a consummate stylist, but also a master of psychology, sucking the Israelites into his web before lashing out at them with devastating potency.

The biblical text is inspiring not only for its structure and language, but also for its content. When that selfsame Amos speaks of God's demand for justice in 5:24, he utters words that resonated in the ears of his auditors. Even if they did not heed his imprecations, they certainly understood the image behind the phrase "Let justice well up as waters and righteousness as a mighty stream." To the people of Amos' hometown of Tekoa, some fifteen miles south of Jerusalem on the northern edge of the desert, the image of a rushing stream cascading through an otherwise dry wadi must have had incredible power. Even today, those of us who have traveled through the Negev will immediate respond to the flood of justice that comes like a torrent of water in a dry creek bed. It's an expression whose impact has lost none of its strength over the last 2,800 years.

Or, one certainly should turn to the words of the Psalms, a collection written by many authors over different times and in different circumstances. Yet virtually everyone knows the Twenty-third psalm; we recognize it by the lilt of the Hebrew poetry, but also because it speaks of timeless promises of hope and security. But just when we are lulled into complacency by the gentle words of the 23rd, we can turn to Psalm 137 for one of the most vicious statements in all of Scripture: "Blessed be they who dash the heads of the [Babylonian] infants against the rocks." This is hardly David, the sweet singer of Israel, but another writer, a man among the exiled Judeans in Babylonia who has, one suggests, seen a similar fate befall his own son or daughter at the hands of invading soldiers. The *chutzpah* of the biblical tradition to include even such a bitter and enraged tirade of legitimate human passion testifies to the honesty of the editors of this text, and that draws me to it with deep admiration and affection, even when I am appalled at some of the actions imagined or actually committed by men and women in the pages of the biblical epic.

I probably ought also to mention that the Bible is just as capable of offending a modern sensibility as inspiring awe and reverence. I have already referred to Psalm 137, but one might also call to mind the story of Saul in 1 Samuel 22 when he murders the priests of Nob, the episode in Genesis 34 when the sons of Jacob slaughter the newly-circumcised men of Shechem, the story of Jepthah who kills his own daughter in Judges 8 and the laws concerning the stubborn and rebellious son in Deuteronomy 21. Each one of these accounts is hard to handle within the ethical framework of a twenty-first century liberal Jew, and the only way that I have been able to cope effectively with them is to affirm that they may have been appropriate in their own time and place, but that they have no role in my personal and contemporary religious philosophy or sensibility.

One could multiply examples manifold, but these should suffice. They indicate the intensity of my attachment to the Bible as a source both of substance, especially ethical insight, and of literary genius. There is nothing primitive about this document, and that is why it has survived millennia as the most read book in the world's history and as the text that has transformed world civilization more than any other.

Anyone who knows me is aware that I am hardly a mystic. My fundamental approach to life and to the religious dimension of life is rationalistic. Yet, when it comes to Torah, there are two instances in which I candidly admit to a very different and nonrational response.

The Torah has been read in public for the last twenty-five hundred years, ever since the days of Ezra and Nehemiah (see his chapter 8). Wherever Jews have gathered for worship—in every place they lived, in every age, under conditions of security, but also in times of great duress—the weekly reading of the Torah has been central. Even in Nazi concentration camps, Jews gathered without a scroll and recalled by memory the verses appropriate to each particular week and holy celebration. Between worship services, they studied the Torah assiduously; it was always a vital part of their lives. When I read the Torah from the *amud* (reading desk), I am intensely conscious of repeating the identical act that Jews have done so many times over the last two and a half millennia. Even more, when I replace the Torah in the ark, I place my hand on it and have a sense of channeling the Jewish generations directly into my consciousness. The *Haggadah* of Passover teaches us that we should learn "retrojection," the skills of throwing ourselves back in time so that we might vicariously experience prior events and challenges and know historical personalities. I grew up during the early days of television, watching John Cameron Swayze host a show called "You Are There," during which historical moments were recreated as though we were actually present. I read Plutarch's *Lives of Notable Greeks and Romans* and Henrik van Loon's biographies of long-dead famous people (also titled *Lives*) and, perhaps my favorite childhood book, Mark Twain's *A Connecticut Yankee in King Arthur's Court*. All of these stimulated a historical imagination that culminates every time I touch the Torah and am immediately transported back in time to Jewish worlds I never experienced, but know with an amazing intimacy from my contact with this scroll. It is an amazingly magical and mystical experience that continues to stun me, both because of its reality and because it is so foreign to the way I approach most aspects of my life.

There is a second mystical experience I have concerning the Torah. In an illuminated niche on the side wall of our main sanctuary in Corpus Christi, we display a "Holocaust Torah." This Torah is on permanent loan from a trust at the Westminster Synagogue in London, a trust that acquired 1564 Czech Torahs that had been confiscated by the Nazis when they invaded that country in 1939. This particular Torah had been taken from the small town of Domazlice (aka Taus), just east of the German-Czech border in Bohemia. The Torah had been stored in a warehouse near Prague, carefully catalogued and labeled, while the Jews of the town were exterminated. After WWII, the Torahs were moved to London and then, over time, "adopted" by congregations around the world. It is among the most precious possessions of our congregation, and we have rolled it to display the fifteenth chapter of Exodus, the poem or song that the Israelites sang when they had survived Pharaoh's oppression and the crossing of the Reed Sea to freedom. It is our way of reminding ourselves that we, in our times, have faced persecution, but we have also survived.

But I have a feeling that it is not only the physical scroll that has come to rest in south Texas. I believe that the souls of all the Jews of Domazlice, the people who read from this Torah every week, that they whose lives were cut mercilessly short, have also migrated to our city and into our congregation. Their presence poses a special challenge to every member of Congregation Beth Israel: as much as you live a Jewish life for yourself, you also have an *alter ego*, the soul of one of the martyrs of Domazlice, and you must live in such a way that you fulfill the truncated life of that person. In many respects, this idea is foreign and outside my "comfort zone," but I find it intensely meaningful, and I am strangely at home with it. Maybe I'm more of a mystic than I thought.

But now to another question. How do I understand this book? Is it God's verbal and infallible revelation, or is it a human document? And if the latter, then why should it play such an important role in the history of human culture and development?

We ought to begin with a few caveats. The Bible is one of the most complex books to read, especially if one does not have a teacher or a commentary as a guide. Consider, for example, that it is not a single document written by a single author but an anthology of different texts, each with a distinctive point of view or multiple points of view. Some books focus more on priestly material, while others tend toward the prophetic. Even then, the various texts were written at different times, under different social and historical influences. These time lapses and new circumstances make it difficult to relate one part of the Bible to another.

The Bible was composed at a time when Jews had an entirely different worldview than that which we have today. Concepts and even individual words took on meanings then that are foreign to us today. For example, the ancients had little difficulty accepting the reality of miraculous interventions in the realm of nature, whereas we inevitably strive to explain away miracles with naturalistic explanations. For them, the splitting of the Reed Sea was not complicated or unacceptable at face value; for us, we wonder if it was not the result of a volcanic eruption on Santorini and the ensuing tidal wave, a great wind or some other cause that does not require God's interruption of the natural sequence of events. Nor did the biblical ancients (or their rabbinic counterparts) have any sense of historical development. The tradition says *Ain Mukdam u-M'uchar baTorah*, nothing precedes in time and nothing follows, but everything occurs simultaneously (*b. Pesahim* 6b). This is a perspective that lasted up to the Italian Renaissance in Western Europe; biblical heroes in fourteenth-century art looked like fourteenth-century Italians, and the Judean landscape looked like Tuscany. People had little or no ability to understand that what went on millennia ago was qualitatively different from the events of their own times.

A good reader of the Bible tries to approach any given section on at least three levels: What did the original author mean in his own time? How have the commentators of the rabbinic and medieval eras understood that section? And, finally, what does it mean to me in my modern world? After all, we have as much right in our own time and circumstances to react to a biblical text as other human beings of various historical eras did in their time—our common humanity gives us that right. (I am indebted to the late Rabbi W. Gunther Plaut for this formulation.)

We also have to ask ourselves if we accept the accounts given in Scripture as reality and fact, or if we read them in other ways. Philo of Alexandria, for example, was not able to accept the idea that God had physical characteristics, so he resorted to allegory whenever there was mention, for example, of God's outstretched arm (not a physical arm, but an expression of divine power). Others have thought of the text in terms of metaphor, while even others have looked beyond the details and asked: "What is the lesson that the Bible is trying to teach? Thus, a person who approaches Genesis 1 in this manner is not concerned with whether the Bible is referring to six days of twenty-four hours or six millennia. What this reader understands is that there is order in the creation and a hierarchy of entities within the physical, animal and human world. This insight does not depend on the details, but on the overall structure and message of the text. Similarly, that one God created everything conveys the ethical lesson that everything within the cosmos is linked together by its single generative source and that, as a consequence, we have a connection and responsibility for all aspects of the creation. Among other things, since the physical world shares the same image of God that inheres in human beings, we are not permitted to trash the world, but must care for it as we would for another human person. In a polytheistic universe, the starving black child in sub-Saharan Africa could be seen as the responsibility of the god of that region, absolving the American worshipper of any responsibility. But, under the biblical and monotheistic formula, that child is related to every other human person and is, therefore, a human being for whom we have social and ethical obligations.

Some Jews (and other religious people) think of the Bible as the given word of God. They read the text of both Exodus 19-20 and 32:18 in a literal manner, understanding that the meeting of Moses and God at the top of Sinai was accompanied by the conveyance of specific content. Orthodox Jews believe that the entire text of the Torah was revealed to Moses during these forty days, but also that he received a second, oral Torah that encompasses all valid interpretations, extensions and applications of the written text of the first five books. This second part of the revelation was eventually reduced to writing, we are told, as the Babylonian Talmud. This oral Torah, then, inerrantly transmitted from Sinai to our own time, possesses the same mandatory authority as the written Torah, and the response of the pious

Jew is to respond, as did the Israelites, "All that the Lord has said, we shall do and we shall obey" (Exod 24:7). The appropriate stance in the face of an explicit divine command is obedience.

I have found this posture impossible to accept. First, there is little that is orthodox in my character or personality; I know myself too well to act with unquestioning obedience. Beyond that, however, my entire approach to the composition of the Torah is that it is a document composed by human beings in many different eras and many different circumstances between approximately 1000 and 500 BCE. Rather than recounting a single divine revelation in about 1250 BCE, the final version of the Torah text reflects a variety of influences, some of which coordinate well with others and some of which seem at odds with different sections of the text. I have never found a methodology for distinguishing between what God may actually have said at Sinai and what human beings added to the narrative in later generations. As a consequence, I respond to the total corpus of biblical literature as the work of human beings, humans inspired by God, to be sure, but still human beings. As a human being of equal in value to the ancients, I (perhaps arrogantly) believe that it is my right and duty to understand what God wants of me in my own time and place, just as the authors of Leviticus and Deuteronomy did in theirs.

I once heard Elie Wiesel speak about two different kinds of people. One was a person who was influenced by the "ism," by the laws and practices of the faith. This person puts the rules and the procedures at the front of his practice. The other type was more responsive to the needs of people and was willing to make adjustments, even in traditional *halacha*, if such were necessary to respond to human situations. A verse from Psalms (119:126) can be liberally translated: "When it is time to work for the Lord, annul even God's law."

During the Vietnam War, I was Dean of HUC-JIR in Cincinnati. When rabbinical students had to wrestle with their reaction to the unpopular war and to potential service as military chaplains, they often turned to me for counsel, and I had to think about my own response. To be sure, I was exempt, having already served in the U.S. Army, but what would I choose if I were in their stead. I quickly came to understand that people and their needs preceded the formal "ism" of Judaism and that I would have volunteered as a chaplain had I been eligible. I could not privilege my rabbinical role and my personal view of the conflict when Jewish men and women were at risk in an area of mortal danger; their welfare was paramount and superseded even my own. Service to others was a cardinal value in my outlook on life and on the rabbinate. I refuse to subordinate the real needs of human beings to some abstract legal principle, especially when the divine provenance of the law is highly suspect.

On the other hand, I do not want to dismiss or diminish the sacred quality of Scripture. If everything is up for discussion, debate and even discard, then what ties me to the history and traditions of our people and our religion? If novelty is all that there is, where is the continuity with the previous generations? I have come to the conclusion that there are in Torah (Torah in its broadest sense, not just the five books, but Jewish lore and learning of all sorts) a number of consistent themes that run through the entire experience of the Jews. Some of these themes are: the existence of God, the value of prayer, the importance of caring for the less fortunate (*tzedaka*), the impact of Israel as a center of gravity, a sense of common destiny for all Jews, various holy days and rituals, the value of education and literacy as a way to understand God's will, the Hebrew language, etc. Each of these themes appears at almost every moment in the Jewish pilgrimage, but often in distinctive manifestations that are conditioned by the historical circumstances and needs. The various themes represent core Jewish values that seem always present in the Jewish experience.

Consider the image of a craft loom. There are weft threads that go from front to back, running through the entire fabric. Then, the weaver slides a shuttle back and forth, across the weft, using warp threads, creating texture, pattern and color. As the tapestry takes shape, it is rolled on a spindle in front of the weaver so that the next inches of the weft may themselves take on the design. For me, the persistent themes of the Jewish experience are the weft, but each generation of Jews casts its own warp and creates its distinctive fabric. How each theme is manifested in a particular setting is a combination of the consistent theme and the idiosyncratic design of that particular situation. Both are there; the fabric cannot be complete without both. And the completed weaving is then rolled forward, as is the entirety of the Jewish past, available to be unrolled and studied whenever a Jew wants to examine it.

A great deal of our understanding of the Torah depends on what we think happened at the top of Sinai. As I mentioned earlier, it is methodologically impossible accurately to separate words that might have been spoken by the Deity and words that were later appended by human authors. Short of maintaining that every word and every letter was spoken or dictated to

Moses by God, we are faced with an unsolvable dilemma. Perhaps all we can be sure of is the final product, whatever its origins and authorship, that has been handed down to us over the centuries

But there is another approach. When I was a junior at Oberlin College, I took a course entitled Modern Religious Thought. Among the books that we read was *I and Thou* by Martin Buber. I confess that at twenty-one years of age his basic message only marginally influenced me. But as I have matured during the past five decades, I began to understand and then deeply to appreciate the implications of Buber's theology of relationship. In particular, I have found that it helps me make sense of the events of Sinai and their sequels.

Buber taught that the essence of the meeting between God and Moses was that they kindled a relationship which we call a covenant. The concept of covenant (*brit*) is central to my understanding of both what happened at Sinai, to the survival of the Jewish people ever since and to my own religious purpose today. The Buberian meeting at Sinai occurred, the sage teaches, without the revelation of content or words; it was a true meeting in which an enduring relationship was established. The rest of Jewish history can be summarized as a collection of answers to this question: "What is required of us to live in such a way as to be worthy of being in covenantal relationship with the most holy entity we can imagine?" Leviticus 19:2 reflects this notion when it challenges the Israelites (and us) to "be holy because the Lord your God is holy." Each generation since Sinai has striven to answer this question, often carrying forward insights from prior times, but always adding a response that fits its own situation and circumstances. Torah, the accumulated Jewish lore and learning, is the cumulative record of Jewish attempts to define how to live a holy life that would dignify the covenant and the God who undergirds it. As a modern Jew, I am called to make my own response to this fundamental question, always conscious of my relationships and obligations to the past, but equally mindful of my debt to the Jewish future.

Some people might object that a document written by human beings, however inspired by their relationship with God, cannot compel allegiance. I take the opposite position. I affirm that a Torah written by God would certainly be a remarkable book, one worthy of being the all-time best seller in the world's history. We ought to assume this of God. But for human beings to have collaborated in the crafting of the Torah with such skill that their product has changed world history more than any other—is not this all the more remarkable and worthy of our highest admiration? I stand in awe of those ancient human authors whose wisdom has amply stood the test of time and whose courage is manifest by their inclusion of passages that were morally challenging and potentially embarrassing, but which they chose not to censor and excise from the religio-national record.

I stand four-square in a tradition that believes that biblical Judaism empowers the human being to be an active partner with the divine. More than twenty-five hundred years ago, the author of Deuteronomy offered the idea that human beings are capable of participating actively in the creation of the covenant. "For this commandment . . . is not too difficult for you, neither is it far off . . . But the word is very near to you, in your mouth and in your heart, that you may do it" (30:11-14). A thousand years later, the Babylonian Talmud (b. BM 59a-b) told the story of a man named Aknai who had an oven that had been contaminated. He adduced all sorts of miracles to prove to the assembled rabbis that his oven could be reassembled and that it would be kosher. But they refused to agree; we do not make *halacha* based on miracles. Finally, a voice from heaven sided with Aknai, but the rabbis demurred and insisted that "ever since the Torah was given, we do not pay attention to a voice from heaven [*bat kol*]." Their point? Human beings are themselves capable of discerning the will of God. How? By study and debate, by using the mental faculties that God has already vouchsafed to us. As a statement of human empowerment, there is nothing better. After all, God agreed with the rabbis. "God laughed and said: 'My children have bested Me.'"

But we are not alone in this quest for a holy life. In fact, I believe that the Bible teaches us that we have been given three vital gifts that make this search both possible and potentially successful. Two of these gifts derive from the third chapter of Genesis. Adam and Eve may have eaten from the tree of the knowledge of right and wrong, good and evil, but in so doing they were given the ability to make those distinctions. The expulsion from Eden puts the two of them in the "real" world where work, pain, interpersonal relationships, and death all must be confronted. But there is a corollary to this change of locale. The corollary is that Adam and Eve must now make ethical and moral decisions on their own; in this new world they have the power not only to make the decisions, but also to enact them. The second divine gift, then, is the power to implement choices, the ability to put one's values into effect.

But, one might ask, how do they know what is right and wrong. Here is the third divine gift: Torah, again in its broadest sense. Over the centuries,

Jews have been given a continuing revelation of how to conduct themselves in the world; we have the record of the choices that Jews made in the past, the values they thought of as holy, their judgments about what constituted a godly and good life. The word *halacha* derives from the Hebrew verb *halach*, meaning to walk. Halacha, then, is a guide to the path that one should walk as one wends one's way through life. So Adam and Eve and their descendants have the ability to know right from wrong, the gift of knowing what constitutes good and evil, and the power to make their choices real in human society. Once these gifts are conveyed to men and women, the rest is up to them; this is the human empowerment of the Torah.

It is very common to refer to the Torah as "law." And, to be sure, there are 613 laws or *mitzvot* contained in the five books, at least according to traditional Jewish reckoning. But these laws do not exhaust the contents of the Torah. It includes a good deal of national history in the form of legends about the founding patriarchs and matriarchs of the Jewish people, some poetry (like Exodus 15 and the various blessings of the tribes) and ethical exhortations (see Lev 19:1-2, for example), among other non-legal materials. "Law" is decidedly inadequate to describe even the Torah in its most restricted sense (just the first five books of the Hebrew Bible) and certainly falls woefully short of making sense of Torah when one thinks of it in its most expansive form: the entirety of the Jewish tradition that begins with the Bible, but never ends.

Torah as law also poses problems for someone like myself who doubts the Mosaic origins of the text and who, therefore, has qualms about the mandatory authority of its statements. Some scholars translate the word "Torah" as "instruction" or "teaching," and I am not uncomfortable with that usage. I appreciate its derivation from the Hebrew trilateral root *yod-resh-hey*, meaning "to throw." Torah is what a teacher throws toward a student, instruction.

But teaching, if it is done well and skillfully, ought also to involve a goal. It seems to me that Torah's goal is a set of expectations based largely on the ethical values enunciated by the biblical prophets.

Jews have characteristically eschewed speculative philosophy and theology, with some rare exceptions, like the Kabbalah and other forms of mysticism. Jews were, of course, intrigued with ideas such as "What will happen to me after I die?" and "What will the messianic future be like?" But they were also skeptical, rationalistic, and worldly enough to wonder how could anyone come up with a satisfactory answer to such quandaries.

They found no methodology that would permit them to respond with any assurance that their answers were correct, so they generally left problems like these to the realm of faith. "I'll find out when it happens, and if I never find out sobeit; that will be the will of God or the way of the world."

So, traditionally, Jews turned their focus to matters which they could affect during their terrestrial lives. "I may not be able to tell you much about the nature of the messiah, but I certainly can distinguish between a righteous person and a scoundrel, between what is right and decent and what is wrong and ugly. I know what kind of behavior to expect from myself and from my neighbors." This approach is sometimes called "orthopraxis" or right practice. It centers on what a human being needs to do in the here-and-now and leaves the speculative side of religion ("orthodoxis" or right belief) to the side.

There is a reason for this focus. Judaism is fundamentally a group process. Its goal is, first and foremost, to create a society where values we associate with God and godliness are put into practice on a daily basis. Obviously, this also involves the creation of righteous individuals, but they are not ends in themselves but means to the expression of Torah values in society. Laws are the ways these values and principles are implemented because laws tell everyone in the society what they have a right to expect from other people. Traffic laws, for example, are cues; they tell us that we are to stop at a red light and go forward on green. Every other driver knows the same code and can, therefore, adjust his or her behavior accordingly. Torah makes a stable and predictable society possible, and that, to my way of thinking, is the earthly goal of the Jewish religion.

I want to conclude this essay on Torah with one of my favorite Hasidic stories. The Maggid of Mezeritch lived from 1704-1772; he was one of the first generation of disciples of the Baal Shem Tov. In one of the most audacious theological statements I have ever read, the Maggid quoted from *Pirke Avot* (2:1): "Know what is above you: an eye that sees, an ear that hears, and all your deeds are inscribed in a book." That is what Yehudah Ha-Nasi said in the second century. But sixteen hundred years later, the Maggid reinterpreted that Mishnaic idea. *Veda*, he said, means "know." *Ma lemala*, that which occurs above you, namely, that which happens in heaven, that which God does. *Mimkha*, depends on you. In other words, God has already acted; God has given you substantial gifts. Now, God is waiting for you to act on those gifts. When you have done your part, then God will again become active and responsive. But, in modern lingo, the ball is in your court.[1] To me, this is the ultimate statement of the notion that we are in charge, that we create our own destiny and are accountable for what we choose to do or not to do. What a daring expression of the partnership between the divine and the human in shaping the future of humanity and the world.

RABBINIC LITERATURE

If the Bible poses problems for the student, rabbinic literature is even more difficult to penetrate. The rabbinic period began with the destruction of the biblical Temple in Jerusalem in 70 CE and continues until the present day. But the heyday of this literature's composition lay between about 200-800 CE. Its source was in the Galilee in the school of Rabbi Judah the Prince, but its period of greatest efflorescence was in the Mesopotamian academies of Sura, Nehardea and Pumbeditha, some three or four centuries later. It spans a transition from Hebrew to Aramaic and a set of circumstances ranging from the aftermath of devastation to the rebuilding of an entire religious civilization. The same methodological challenges that confront the student of the Bible face the student of the much more vast rabbinic literature.

To talk about the Babylonian Talmud (hereafter referred to as BT) as a Reform Jewish rabbi is difficult and somewhat embarrassing. The instruction I received as a seminarian hardly cracked open "the sea of the Talmud," and both we students and the faculty knew it. At best, we had a passing familiarization with this genre of halachic literature that is so crucial to more traditional Jews. There are good reasons for this prioritization of the seminary curriculum. Considering that reality, I suspect that most Reform Jewish rabbis have a sense of inadequacy and inauthenticity when they compare themselves to more traditional rabbis and to the centuries during which the BT has been the controlling document of Jewish life, virtually the exclusive measure by which Jewish leadership qualifications were judged.

On a practical level, Reform Jewish rabbis are rarely asked to answer talmudic questions. Dedicating enough time to change talmudic novices into talmudic scholars would demand an enormous sacrifice of other foci in the rabbinic training program, the omission of subject matter much more directly relevant to the actual functions that Reform Jewish rabbis are required to perform. This represents a very pragmatic judgment on the part

1. Elie Wiesel, *Souls on Fire* (New York: Random House, 1972), 68.

of those who are tasked with and dedicated to providing the movement with effective rabbinic leadership.

There are more theoretical reasons for this professional and academic choice. A great deal has to do with textual authority. Traditional Jews believe that the Torah as it exists today is identical with the Torah that was revealed to Moses at Sinai. Every word, every letter, every space—they all descend directly and accurately from that climactic moment. But the content communicated by God to Moses was not exhausted by the written Torah. Rather, it is contended, an oral Torah was also revealed; the BT is alleged to be that oral Torah. But this premise depends on an *a priori* decision that what happened at Sinai was the revelation of content. This is *a priori* because how one judges the accuracy and authenticity of claims made within the text itself (i.e., God wrote or dictated the words) depends entirely on the values with which one initially approaches the text. As I indicated above in the essay on the Bible, there is credible evidence that questions, if not refutes, the Sinaitic authenticity of the entire Torah. And, if the authority of the original document is called into question, then the subsidiary authority claim of the oral Torah is all-the-more suspect. The modern scholarly evaluation of both the written and oral Torahs, scholarship to which Reform Jewish rabbis generally subscribe, makes it virtually impossible to use the BT as the unimpeachable authority for Jewish religion in the way that traditional Judaism proposes.

Another reason why the Talmud plays a lesser role in liberal Judaism in that decisions codified in sixth-century Mesopotamia emerged in a society so completely different from our own that their relevancy is highly to be questioned. Even if one only claims that the Talmud represents human interpretations, applications and extensions of the written Torah and that from it one can learn about Jewish life during many centuries and in many places, the direct applicability of Talmudic dicta is nonetheless diminished in liberal Judaism. Traditional Jews apply Talmudic concepts and values by using a variety of (sometimes convoluted and intricate) techniques, the most common of which is reasoning by analogy. Liberal Jews prefer to make religious decisions by a more direct and modern-contextual process, even though this means that we have separated ourselves from the classic process of historical Judaism.

I candidly admit that the talmudic reasoning process (if not its substantive content) has at times been useful. The intellectual discipline of wading through complex issues has become part of the strategic make-up of many Jews who have found it a decided advantage when competing with those who do not have this background. But I have also known of Jews who have used talmudic casuistry to excuse or ignore immoral or even criminal behavior. It's a sword with edges that cut in many directions.

There is yet one more significant consideration in the decision by liberal rabbis to downplay the importance of the BT in their daily functioning. Traditional Judaism asserts that the BT contains the sole authority necessary to make every decision required of a Jew, both historically and today. Liberal Jews reject that proposition and believe that there exist extra-talmudic sources of knowledge and wisdom that are as valuable in making contemporary decisions as are those that are contained in ancient documents. It is, of course, important to be aware of the values and precedents brought forward by traditional texts, but liberal Jews deny the proposition that the contents of the BT alone can control our current practice.

Liberal Judaism is not a legalistic form of Judaism. I previously mentioned the insights I garnered from Psalm 119:126 and from Elie Wiesel. We base our guidance to those who ask for it on more than the *halacha* (Jewish law) derived from the BT and its successor legal documents. But there is a second part of the BT, and that element is called *aggada*. *Aggada* is sometimes called midrash, and it contains anecdotes, ethics, values, theology, and philosophy, mythic legends, fables, and a host of other non-legal materials. The midrashic literature is copious; it far exceeds the BT. Some of it is of dubious relevance to us moderns, coming as it does from conditions and societies from different from our own.

But often enough the midrash contains insights that can be easily applied to our contemporary life. These applications depend on the conviction that human life has not radically changed over the last several thousand years. I am convinced that the same basic needs drive human behavior for us as for our ancestors: the desire for survival, food, and shelter; wanting to be surrounded by others who will love and protect us and whom we can love and protect in return; a sense that what we do with our lives is somehow meaningful, valuable and purposeful; and a need to feel a part of something larger than ourselves—a clan, a family, a community or, perhaps, God and God's plan. How we make these drives manifest in our lives may differ from age to age; technological advances have certainly changed, for example, how we grow, gather and use food, but the basic striving to nourish ourselves persists. Midrashic lessons that can be related to these continuing human needs are, therefore, timeless.

Let me offer two of my favorite examples (from among many) to illustrate the usefulness of midrash. Both arise from the story of the Golden Calf in Exodus 32. In the first, the effort is made to exculpate Aaron and to remove from him the guilt of creating the idolatrous statue. After all, who would want the progenitor of Israel's priesthood to be tainted with the stain of idolatry? Thus, we read:

> Rabbi Jeremiah said: "When they brought the nose rings, Aaron raised his eyes to heaven and said: 'To You I lift my eyes, Who is enthroned in heaven. (Ps. 123:1) You know all the thoughts and that against my will I am going to do this.' He threw the gold into the fire, whereupon the Egyptian magicians came and performed their secret arts . . . A calf came out, shaking and leaping" (b. Shabbat 89a).

I have never met a child (including myself many years ago) and even many adults who have not attempted to shift blame for a misdeed to another person or to some abstract force. On the 1970s' TV show, "That Was The Week That Was," Geraldine (played by Flip Wilson) was fond of exclaiming "The devil made me do it." And how many children have had imaginary playmates upon whose shoulders the responsibility for every negative action rested? Or, is it not common today among adults at all levels of accountability to shift blame by declaring "I was just following the rules and the policies." The midrash about Aaron speaks to just such situations.

A second selection also deals with Aaron's guilt, but it adds an additional theme.

> Why was it appropriate to specify the exodus from Egypt? Moses said: "Lord of the Universe, from where did You bring them out? From Egypt, where everybody worshipped animals."
>
> Rav Huna said in the name of Rabbi Yochanan: "This is compared to a wise person who opened a perfume shop for his son on a street of prostitutes. The street did its part, as did the business and the lad, like any youth, also did his share, thereupon falling into evil ways. The father came and caught him with a prostitute. He began screaming, saying: "I'm going to kill you!" His good friend was there, and he said to the father: "You destroyed the youth, and yet you yell at him? You ignored all other professions except perfumery, and you ignored all other streets and only opened a store on a street of prostitutes." [What did you expect?]
>
> Thus, Moses said: "Lord of the Universe, You ignored all the rest of the world, enslaving Your children only in Egypt, where they worshipped animals. Your children learned from them, and

they too have made a calf." Therefore, Scripture says " . . . which You brought out of the land of Egypt." Bear in mind the place from which You brought them out (*Shemot Rabba* 43:7)

It is important to remember that this audacious theological statement is roughly 1800 years old; it is not the creation of some latter-day skeptic or atheist but of an ancient scholar whose theological credentials were impeccably orthodox. And yet here he is, transferring responsibility away from Aaron, Moses, and the entire people directly to God. Should we not be astounded? At base this ancient wise man reminds us of a fundamental lesson: every action has its consequences, so, if you don't think you're going to like the consequences, perhaps you should desist from the action itself. This rule of accountability applies from what we may say casually at a social gathering to leading a nation into international conflict and to just about everything in between.

The collected midrash is the repository of instructive insights like these. There is, to be sure, a great deal of the midrash that liberal Jews would find hard to apply and even distasteful. The misogyny of the ancient world is, for example, fully present in some of these ancient texts, but we would hardly want to make it part of our modern-day teaching. Yet it is difficult to read through even a chapter of *aggada* without coming across a lesson that has retained its ethical and moral value over the centuries.

Thus, as problematic as it is for a liberal Jew to make use of the halachic elements of the BT and the rest of the legal rabbinic literature, when we turn to the *aggada* we find among its pages sources of ongoing inspiration and joyful exploration.

4

Israel: People and/or Nation

IT MIGHT SEEM VERY strange to begin a discussion of what Israel can mean to someone like myself at the corner of 50th and Dorchester Streets on the southside of Chicago in the 1910s or at 1005 Woodland Road in southeastern downtown Cleveland in the same years, but there, trust me, is where the story really begins.

My maternal grandparents lived in a majestic brownstone near the campus of the University of Chicago. My grandfather bore the unmistakable German-Jewish name of Ignatz Hermann Freund (usually referred to as I. H. for understandable reasons). His grandparents had come from south-central Germany and had quickly integrated themselves into the *deitsch* elite of the city. The city directory listed him as a manufacturer. His status was unaltered by the fact that his mother was a full-blooded Sephardic Jewess whose family had moved from Barranquilla, Colombia when her father was appointed consul-general in Detroit. She could trace her lineage back in an unbroken line to 1492.

In Cleveland, the Roseman clan lived on Woodland Avenue, about ten blocks away from the Roseman-Stern Coffee Company that they had founded. Boxes of coffee, tea, baking soda, baking powder, and other condiments filled the shelves of their little business. These more recent immigrants from two *Galitzianer* villages in the Carpathian Mountains of Slovakia were of much more modest status, though Grandpa Ben was as determined as the Freunds that his three sons and a daughter would all have an American university education and then make successes of their lives in the New World. They did.

What united these two seemingly disparate families was their vehement adherence to Reform Judaism as it was practiced between the two World Wars. "Classical Reform Judaism" asserted that being Jewish was being a member of a religious faith only and that the ethnic and nationalistic elements that one might find in historic iterations of Jewish identity had no role or place in America. Jews were Americans by nationality and Jews only by their religious choice. As Rabbi David Philipson famously exclaimed at the 1897 meeting of the Union of American Hebrew Congregations, "America is our Zion." In 1824, Gustav Poznanski, at the dedication of Beth Elohim in Charleston, South Carolina, had made a similar assertion: "This country is our Palestine, this city our Jerusalem, this house of God our temple."

Classical Reform Judaism opposed the creation of a specifically Jewish state: our homeland, they asserted, is wherever we choose to settle. They were, during this era, petrified by the so-called charge of divided or dual loyalty; "if the United States and Palestine/Israel were in conflict with each other, to which side would you be loyal?" The assumption behind the question was that Jews could not be trusted as loyal Americans and that, perhaps, their ultimate affinity lay with some kind of international cabal. And yet, a passionate humanitarian concern for the Jewish victims of tsarist persecution and pogrom led some to support the nascent American Zionist movement to establish a place of refuge, especially as the open door of American immigration policy closed in the 1920s. "We do not need Israel for ourselves; it will be for 'them.'"

Classical Reform Judaism should certainly be seen as an understandable reaction to an American society that was increasingly anti-Semitic and xenophobic. By 1924, American immigration policy had tightened, and the heyday of mass migration to this country had ended. Jews were excluded from higher-level positions in a variety of companies (e.g., Ford Motor Co., Proctor and Gamble) and even from entire professions (e.g., the diplomatic corps, elite law firms, surgery); individual academic institutions attempted to enforce quotas on Jewish admissions; Jews were denied accommodations at hotels, resorts, and restaurants. Isolationism governed foreign relations, and economic fear, born of the trauma of the Great Depression, led to a variety of discriminatory practices. Before WWII, something more than half of the American population were willing to respond to a survey and affirm that they did not like or trust Jews. In such an environment, it made sense to many American Jews to structure their religious credo so that it would appear maximally in line with the predominant views and practices of American Protestantism. This would enhance their acceptance into American society. Thus, some congregations actually switched their main service to Sunday, although some saw the adoption of Sunday worship as an unwarranted and demeaning pandering in search of Christian-American approval. One congregation in St. Louis even split when some of its members and its rabbi decided permanently to celebrate Hanukkah on December 25th. The rabbis preferred the title "Doctor"; Hebrew was minimized and Yiddish forbidden; distinctive Jewish ritual clothing was abandoned, as were dietary laws and other practices that might have had the effect of setting Jews apart from their Gentile neighbors and, in the mind of Classical Reform Jews, of encouraging anti-Semitism.

So it is hardly surprising that young adult Jews emerging from this milieu would eschew Jewish particularism and focus their religious commitments on the universal ethical and moral mandates of the biblical prophets. Classical Reform Judaism arose in part as a response to negative dimensions prevalent in American society, but also to several positive virtues that they shared with much of the general American populace. They believed that

- Human beings can affirmatively control their lives. Through laws, carefully thought-through and planned institutions and social structures and concerted civic action, we can dictate the direction that society should and will take.

- Even though some religions teach about human depravity, there existed a fundamental core of goodness in every person. This view of human character was essentially positive and optimistic.

- And that human society was ineluctably heading toward a wonderful golden age of messianic perfection. They read Hegel's philosophy, but added to his ideas the notion that each new synthesis would be better than its predecessor. The future would be glorious, and progress was inevitable.

The mantra of the years between the wars, for Classical Reform Jews and for their gentile American counterparts had been coined by a French psychologist Émile Coué. In 1920 Coué's strategy was published in English in a book entitled *Self-Mastery Through Conscious Auto-Suggestion*. His catch-phrase for self-improvement was "Every day in every way I'm getting better and better." In the U.S., the celebrated preacher Norman Vincent Peale made this adage into an article of optimistic faith for liberal-thinking Americans, and for the Jews who fell into their way of thinking.

Events, however, rarely follow the script, as well-intentioned and as well-thought-out as it might be. The ideals that characterized Classical Reform Judaism (and its Protestant equivalent, the Social Gospel movement) came under attack over the course of twenty years in the middle of the twentieth century.

The first assault came against the notion that we could control our own affairs and dictate our destiny. In November 1929, the bottom fell out of the stock market and the economy of the nation (and of the world) crashed. The hubris that pretended to control was undermined by the Great Depression. It became clear that we could not control even one segment of human activity, the economy, much less the entire scope of human endeavor.

WWII destroyed the facile and naïve notion that human beings are essentially good. As the reports of the death squads and murderous concentration camps filtered out of Central Europe, the potential for bestial and evil behavior by otherwise "normal" people made it difficult to uphold the idea of fundamental human decency. Since the early 1940s, we have been wrestling with new constellations of character and personality, many of which affirm that there are dimensions of ourselves that are potentially good, but other sides that can be evil, and that we need to balance the two and make righteous choices. This trend was mirrored in the works of the great Protestant theologian, Reinhold Niebuhr, who spoke of Christian realism and the existence of a real thing called evil. No one is prepared in the modern, post-Holocaust world, to assert that human character is wholly positive and constantly striving for a blessed and righteous outcome.

The third pillar of Classical Reform Jewish faith maintained that we are headed toward a future of universal messianism. My maternal grandmother could not, for example, understand why I would want to devote my life to the service of one small group of the human species, when humanity as a whole beckoned for my involvement. Though she was proud of her grandson and his achievements, she never varied from her conviction that universal involvement always superseded commitment to the welfare of some subspecies on the planet.

Thus it was nearly traumatic on May 14, 1948, four days after my ninth birthday, that our family were sitting at dinner at our home on Albemarle Street in Washington, DC when the news of Israel's independence broke. Though I did not comprehend my parents' reaction fully for many years, I have a vivid memory of the *tone* of their conversation that evening.

What was traumatic about that evening was that it forced my parents and Jews who had been raised like them to confront a difficult truth; they suddenly realized that aspects of their Jewish identity that they thought they had eliminated from their psychic make-up were, in fact, barely repressed below a veneer of quasi-assimilation. The establishment of the State of Israel forcibly stripped away the pretensions of universalism and demanded that they deal with what only recently had been unthinkable: they were Jews who in some as yet unexplored, but very deep and powerful ways, were tied to that people and its national expression. Trying to harmonize these emerging sentiments with their Classical background became one of the projects that occupied them for the rest of their lives. Mom died in 1973 and Dad in 1974, both in their early sixties. Because I never lived under their roof after June 1956, we had scant opportunity to probe the course of this re-examination. But it was obvious from many subtle signals that their relationship to Zionism forever thereafter provoked their concern and attention.

So far, all of this represents the background that I brought into my twenties. Lots of experience living overseas but virtually nothing that would guide me in reformulating attitudes about Israel that had been conceived originally in a Classical Reform Jewish home. Whatever religious school education I had as a teen was focused on social action, and Oberlin College in the late 1950s had no courses on the history of Zionism or modern Israel. One might imagine that this would have changed when I enrolled in the rabbinical program at Hebrew Union College-Jewish Institute of Religion in Cincinnati, but not so. For two reasons. The history of Israel and Zionism was taught as only one topic among many in a course on modern Jewish history, but primarily from a historical perspective. Contemporary Israel was not a subject in the curriculum. Beyond that fact, however, the approach of the faculty followed the *Wissenschaft* model of learning. Somewhat facetiously, this might be termed the photographic theory of education: first you make an exposure and then you wait to see what develops. Each discipline was taught as a discrete entity, and there was no mechanism to help student create a synthetic, integrated whole in which the meaning of the topic would be salient. This was true, not solely with regard to Israel, but for every subject. (Parenthetically, this is probably no longer true with regard to Israel. Since fall 1970, all students have spent their first graduate year in Jerusalem, an experience that may force them to develop a point of view regarding the Jewish state.)

OF TRIBES AND TRIBULATIONS

I made my first trip to Israel in January of 1971, partly to meet with the students and partly to tour the country. That visit prepared me for change, but the real impetus for growth came in October 1973 when the forces of Egypt and its allies attacked Israel on Yom Kippur. I vividly recall standing at a communal rally at Temple Sholom in Cincinnati and being appalled at the prospect that Israel might cease to exist. What was this place that seemed to have such a powerful emotional hold on me? Since that time I have returned to Israel every five years or so, occasionally leading congregational tour groups, and I have come to a richer and multifaceted appreciation of the Jewish state.

Let me say without equivocation that I am a Zionist. Not in the classical sense that asserts that a Jew must live in Israel completely to fulfill one's identity. I am a Zionist, like most American Jews, because I firmly support Israel's right to exist in safety, because I admire the miracles that its citizens have wrought under difficult circumstances, and because I treasure the historical connections that are possible when one walks in the actual footsteps of biblical luminaries. And, most of all, because I am convinced and determined that there must be at least one country on the earth where a Jew can find refuge and security as a matter of right. When I was rabbi at Temple Beth El in Madison, WI, a member of the synagogue, Fred Leyser, told me of his experience as a passenger on the German steamship, *The Saint Louis*. Armed with what they believed to be valid entry visas for Cuba, 938 Jews left Hamburg and journeyed across the Atlantic. Cuba refused to honor the visas, and the ship and its passengers rode at anchor in Havana harbor while efforts were made to find an alternative refuge. Eventually, the ship steamed back to Europe, passing within eyesight of the lights of Miami. Of the passengers, only those who disembarked at Southampton survived the next few years. I am convinced that *The Saint Louis* affair was a deliberate test of Western governments to ascertain their interest in Jewish refugees. When no nation would accept even a few bedraggled passengers, Hitler knew that no one would lift a hand to oppose The Final Solution. If we learned one lesson from the Holocaust, we learned that Jewish lives may never again be a political pawn to be used at the whim of other people.

I was blessed, in a perverse sense, by not being indoctrinated in the pre-state Zionist myth. In that idyll, every settler looked like Sal Mineo playing Ari ben Canaan in the movie *Exodus*, while other kibbutzniks danced the hora wearing quaint blue and white caps. It was a vision of the creation of an earthly paradise, a healthy, vibrant society in which everyone was joyous and satisfied, where there were no persecutions and no social problems. Many diaspora Jews who had been brought up with this romantic vision were deeply disappointed when reality turned out to be far distant from what they imagined. Israel never could have matched the propagandistic image that was conveyed by its most ardent proponents; it was a real country with real, flesh-and-blood citizens who behaved like most other human beings.

Except they did not. They went about creating a unique human society, imperfect to be sure, but as remarkable as any nation-building experiment has ever been. The founders and builders of the state quickly transcended the rabbinic bromides that Jerusalem possesses nine of the ten measures of beauty in the world and that the very air of Israel makes one wise. The dreams of a homeland, fantasized in Russian shtetls and Polish ghettos, crashed against the stark realities of organizing a brand-new society on the desperately barren soil at the eastern end of the Mediterranean, all the while under ferocious attack from hostile neighbors, disease, and deprivation. What they achieved is nothing short of miraculous and heroic.

What one thinks of immediately when one speaks of Israeli heroism are the Israel Defense Forces. The battle cry of Masada, "Never again," has been implemented with enormous skill, courage, and sacrifice. Of that there is no doubt; the state would not exist today, had the IDF failed.

Yet, to my way of thinking the IDF is only one element of what makes Israel unique. In fact, I am often impatient when the fundraisers trot out another general or so-called defense expert to present Israel's situation to American communal gatherings. I know that threats of annihilation open checkbooks, but Israel's uniqueness is so much vaster than its military prowess. Almost every nation has an army (except, for example, Costa Rica); the IDF is good but hardly unique among the world's military establishments. I think of Israel as far more than an embattled, armed camp. I focus on other aspects of Israel's remarkable achievements.

No other country has tried to build a national culture while it took in a mass immigration from roughly seventy countries around the world. What they had in common was that they called themselves Jews, but there the similarities ended. There is a midrash that says that God collected dust from all different locations of the world and mixed it all together when He prepared to form the first man so that no race or national group could claim superiority (b. Sanhedrin 38b). Consider just a fraction of this challenge. How does one create a cohesive nation, a sense of common purpose and unity, when the components of the population are as disparate as Holocaust survivors smuggled surreptitiously by B'richa out of European displaced persons camps, American middle-class, suburbanite Jews, B'nai Israel from India, Yemenite Jews from pre-modern Arabian villages, secular former Communists from the Soviet Union, but also fervent Hasidic Jews from around the world? The relocation of Ethiopian Jews from conditions of extermination is the only case of modern history where a black population has been moved for purposes other than enslavement. But how do you integrate them into a largely white, twentieth-century civilization? It's really little short of miraculous, and this is the story of Israel that never ceases to awe and impress me. The State of Israel is the most fascinating social laboratory in the world and, by and large, one of the most successful.

It is also a nation that has compiled an unequaled technological record. Jews have never made their mark in the world because of numbers or great physical presence. Nor are they ever likely to do so. From biblical times, this little people pioneered exalted ethical and moral standards that changed every subsequent world civilization. In more modern times, Jews have made their marks through intellectual striving and technological innovation. Consider only one datum. During the twenty years from 1980 to 2000, Israel's Arab neighbors registered 367 patents in the United States. Israel recorded 7,652, roughly twenty-one times as many. These discoveries range across the entire technical spectrum and have revolutionized such disparate fields as medicine, manufacturing, and defense. As much as we all know that a strong military defense is essential for Israel, it is this record of intellectual achievement that elicits my highest level of admiration and enthusiasm for today's Israel.[1]

I realize that my background has fundamentally influenced my outlook. I grew up in a home that was not ritualistically observant, but where the ideals of the biblical prophets were taken very seriously. Both of my parents had social work training, and both of them were fully committed to the relief of suffering and to the building of societies where human character and personality could flourish. For a number of years, my father served as the American Permanent Representative (ambassador) to the small agencies of the United Nations headquartered in Geneva, including the International Refugee Organization (now known as the U.N. High Commission

1. For more background, read Dan Senor and Saul Singer, *Start-Up Nation: The Story of Israel's Economic Miracle* (New York: Twelve/Hachette, 2009). The data cited above are from pages 209-10.

for Refugees). The dinner table at our home in Cologny was the frequent site of long discussions by some of the world's most notable thinkers and doers about how to aid distressed populations. I imbibed this heady elixir during my adolescent years, and it has certainly stayed with me through the rest of my life. Charles Jordan, the head of the American Jewish Joint Distribution Committee, was a frequent dinner guest and, even though my father represented American interests, not Jewish ones, solutions to the plight of European Jewish refugees were common grist for discussion. When I think about the phrase *Am Yisrael*, I am drawn to its sense of "the people Israel" rather than "the nation Israel." The humanitarian impulse is just too deeply ingrained in me to do otherwise.

More than the technical and medical achievements of which Israel can boast with pride—and they are truly remarkable—Israel has overcome external threats to produce a vibrant culture of literature and poetry, of art, of music (e.g., the Israel Philharmonic), of theater (consider the theater of the deaf and blind in old Jaffa and Habima Theater), and exemplary social services. I cannot go to Israel without a mandatory stop at Yad Lakashish (The hand extended to the elderly), a sheltered workshop of the most humane kind. All but one of our eleven grandchildren wear *tallitot* from there; the other's tallit is from the Women of the Wall. A country that makes provision for its less-fortunate citizens, even at a time of military threat, is worthy of considerable admiration.

Perhaps the most significant impact Israel has had on me is as a corrective to the Classical Reform Jewish upbringing of my youth. That manifestation of Judaism was essentially cerebral and intellectual. Emotion was largely absent from its services, as was poetry, chanting, davening (the involvement of the entire body in prayer), specifically Jewish music (unless you think of Mozart and Schumann as Jewish musicians), singing, and, generally, congregational involvement. The people on the pulpit were the actors, and the people in the pews were the passive audience.

Beginning in the early 1950s, this constellation of Jewish practices began to change. The UAHC camps that I attended in those years were hugely instrumental in fostering new styles, but at base I credit Israel as the stimulus that ended the period of Classical Reform and inaugurated the modern era when many of the former trends were reversed. Chief among those influences was the Six-Day War of 1967 which revolutionized the character of American Reform Judaism. It was only after 1967 that many changes entered Reform Jewish practice. Among these new ritual practices, *kippot* and *tallitot* appeared in Reform temples, albeit only after significant controversy; the breaking of the glass and the use of a *Huppah* became part of Reform weddings; Reform Jews went from a lukewarm relationship to Israel to the founding of an official Reform Jewish Zionist organization; and pork products and shellfish were finally completely eliminated from Temple kitchens. Thanks in large measure to the religio-cultural influences emanating from Israel, the religious and spiritual environment in which a young Jew grows up today are vastly different from those of my childhood. And if our young people are different, so too are older, senior-citizen Jews—like me. What a difference a little sliver of land many thousands of miles away has made!

5

We Were There, Too: Jewish History

To be a Jew means that one is always something of an historian. I've often wondered whether there is an element inherent in being Jewish that urges an involvement with the past. Of course, not every Jew is equally fascinated with the long-ago. Maimonides (1135–1204, Spain and Egypt) thought that "history was a waste of time" (commentary to Mishnah Sanhedrin 10:1), but only a few centuries later Jews who had fled from the Spanish Inquisition undertook historical investigations to understand the dislocative calamity that had occurred to them. Their volumes, *Shevet Yehudah* and *Emek Habakhah*, were not historical writing as we think of it today. They were, rather, a theology of history, attempting to comprehend the expulsion from Iberia as a meaningful part of some divine intent and plan. The German word for this kind of analysis is *Heilsgeschichte*, the historical narrative told from the point of view of its divine purpose. As such, it is based on a few general principles, and specific events must fit into the pre-established matrix. Nonetheless, even though this is not our kind of historical writing, we can observe the growth of a very real historical consciousness among the refugees: they turned to their past to explain their present.

In fact, one need not focus on the Middle Ages in Christian Europe or in Muslim lands to find the roots of historical interest among Jews. In two places in the book of Deuteronomy, we find directives to be involved with the study of the past. Chapter 4:32 recommends that one search through the past history of God's involvement with the Israelites in order to apprehend the greatness and uniqueness of the God of Israel. This review of history is further highlighted in 32:7 where the text reads: "Remember the days of old, consider the years of ages past; ask your parent, who will inform you, your elders who will tell you." Elsewhere (Psalm 126), the entire history of Israel from Egyptian slavery to the entry into the Promised Land is rehearsed, and one could multiply examples from the biblical text manifold.

The Jewish concern with history comes to an early climax with the writings of Flavius Josephus during the first century CE, after the Hasmonean revolt of 168-165 BCE and the Roman invasion of Judea. In three related books (*The Antiquities of the Jews*, *The Wars of the Jews*, and *Contra Apion*), Josephus set out on a self-conscious mission to preserve the history of his biblical predecessors. He was particularly concerned that the chaotic conditions of his times not obliterate the historical record of his people, and, while his narrative cannot be verified by modern standards of evidence, it is certainly the best and almost the only one we have of this early intertestamental period.

Only two centuries after Josephus wrote his monumental works, a Christian historian named Eusebius sought to chronicle the events of the emerging Church. In *Ecclesiastical History*, the author describes the birth and formation of the new religious movement. But he has some very strong disclaimers when he speaks to the value of history. Jesus (some interpreters understand this as referring to God), he says, quoting the New Testament in Revelation 21:6 and 22:13, is the alpha and the omega, the first and the last, the beginning and the end. History, Eusebius says, always involves change and novelty. But, if Jesus (or God) is the entirety and the perfect vehicle for human experience, then any change must necessarily be away from the sacred ideal and would, therefore, be altogether undesirable. So Eusebius cautions his reader not to become obsessed with history, but to focus on the complete and final salvation that has already and finally been revealed. Nothing more need ever be added to the historical record, Eusebius states, and one has the impression of listening to a second-century avatar of Henry Ford opining that "history is bunk."

Protestant Christianity, especially, looks back to the apostolic age of Christian development. Part of that is motivated by the Lutheran polemic that the medieval Catholic Church had subverted the true meaning of original and pristine Christian teaching and belief; if only one could return to the true beginnings, the faithful would be able to practice the faith as it was meant to be observed. The life, death and resurrection of Jesus was *the* revelatory event beyond which there would be and need be no other. If there were to be an interest in history, it would only be to focus on the essential nature of this disclosure of the key to salvation. But there is little attention given to events or personalities that followed, since they could add nothing to the original and all-important revelation through the Christ.

It is worthy of note that the terminology that the Hebrew Bible uses to refer to the Israelites is exclusively ethnic and social. Terminology counts. What a group calls itself makes a difference. The most common appellation for the Israelites in the Bible is *am*, "people," and less often its parallel, *goi*, "nation." Nearly as prevalent is the phrase *b'nai Yisrael/Ya'akov*, "the children of Israel/Jacob." Together these terms occur hundreds of times, while alternatives appear far less frequently. The word *kahal*, "congregation," is occasionally used, as is the term *eydah*, "assembly."

In the New Testament, the proportions are reversed, so that *kahal* and *eydah* are the chosen Hebrew synonyms for "church." That the early Christians chose to refer to themselves by a different vocabulary and soon switched from Hebrew to Greek also implies a new valuation for them of historical events and processes. In a highly meaningful and symbolic statement, the new church abandoned the Jewish Sabbath day, which represented the conclusion of God's creative process and sought a distinctive identity by proclaiming a different Sabbath day. The new day, the first day of the Jewish week, spoke to the Christian conviction that a new era had dawned and that anything that had transpired in the past was but preparation for this new order of salvation.

The implications of this difference in terminology became poignantly clear to me when I was the rabbi of Temple Beth El in Madison, WI. In the 1970s and early 1980s, the country of Lebanon was wracked by a civil war and repeated massacres of both Shiite Muslims and Maronite Christians. At lunch one day, I asked my Christian colleagues why there had been no public outcry from local churches over the deaths of thousands of Christians. Underlying my question was my conviction that, if even a few of the remaining Jews of Lebanon had been assaulted, vehement sermons would have been preached from nearly all pulpits, Jewish communities across the North American continent would have held protest meetings, sent delegations with petitions to Washington, and engaged in raising special relief funds. But in this case, a case I imagined to be analogous, nothing was happening. Why were there no responses? Our discussion lasted for a long time, but the upshot was the conclusion that being Christian and being Jewish are not the same. The former has to do with a loose community of faith in which members do not feel an integral relationship to each other, while the latter are related by ties of family and kinship—they are a people, not a religion.

A similar situation prevailed between the 1960s and the end of the Iron Curtain in Eastern Europe. Jews in the Soviet bloc were oppressed and persecuted. So were members of other religious groups, even the Russian Orthodox, based on the anti-religious, atheistic ideology of the Communist Party. It is likely that the fate of Jews was worse than others' because of the long tradition of Russian anti-Semitism, but certainly the conditions faced by all religious sects were hardly favorable. Baptists were treated especially badly. Yet the only worldwide protest movement came from Jewish communities throughout the world. Again, one wonders why outrage about this persecution was raised only from one platform and not on behalf of all oppressed co-religionists.

There is an immense difference between an *ethnos* and an *ecclesia*. Those who belong to the former understand themselves to be members of a group that relies on time and place for its continued existence. These characteristics are essential constitutive elements of any historical consciousness; to be an *am* demands involvement in history.

To define oneself or one's group in terms of ethnicity means that theology, philosophy, and religious ritual may rank among the determinative variables, but below the top of the list. Instead, homeland, language, humor, food, a familial sense of common destiny, a willingness and a sense of obligation to care for others of similar background, and even to engage in "family" fights rate higher in terms of self-definition. Homeland, in particular, plays a significant role for Jews. Once immigrants and their children spoke of themselves in terms of the specific place from which their immediate family had emigrated; one described himself or herself as an *Ashkenazi* or a *Sephardi*, as *Poylisch* or *Yeki* or *Galitzianer* or *Litvak*. In the New World, mutual assistance organizations were organized based on places of shared European origin, and the deceased were buried with others of common geographical roots. Today, as immigrant beginnings fade into the fourth or fifth generation, the place that Jews always regarded as their virtual-historical homeland and now-real national center, Israel, focuses this sense of ethnic identity. In the land of Israel, ethnic identity, supplemented by religious consciousness, evokes a powerful historical awareness and images of self that traverse four millennia of Jewish connection with the soil and the stones of that locale. Geography is an important constituent of ethnic identity and its history; Israel functions as that component for Jewish identity.

There is another reason why Christianity has downplayed historical consciousness. The universal church contains peoples of many disparate backgrounds. The only history that they share is the Gospel narrative. Their individual and personal stories are potentially at odds with each other; their historical trajectories are more likely to produce conflict and disunity than a sense of commonality. Several places in the New Testament (see Gal 3:28, Col 3:11, and Rom 10:12) posit the obliteration of personal history by stating "There is neither Jew nor Greek; there is neither bond nor free; there is neither male nor female, for all are one in Christ Jesus." As the church expanded into new regions and absorbed new populations, what served to unify Christianity was the ahistorical, theological document that chronicled the foundational revelation.

The Roman Catholic tradition has more opportunity to be interested in history. The earthly church has an ongoing experience expressed through the Papacy, the lives of the saints, canon law, and the various teachings and pronouncements of the Church. It does seem to me, as an outsider, that these phenomena have the potential to engender a notion of historical consciousness among thoughtful communicants, at least in the sense that the contemporary Catholic can understand himself or herself as part of a two thousand year old and continuing tradition.

Richard Dawkins, the British scientist, calls himself "a cultural Anglican." There may be elements of the ethnic in some nationally based Christian groups, such as the various Orthodox churches and the Maronites. As a general rule, however, the leveling and homogenizing tendencies within modern society—and modern American society, in particular—work to eliminate these characteristics among all groups, Jews included.

This difference may be summarized most succinctly by the opposite responses to a question: "May one be an atheist and still be a member of this group?" To be a Christian means unquestionably to affirm a set of theological propositions, often abbreviated as creedal statements; failing to subscribe to those religious propositions, one may not legitimately claim to be a Christian. To the contrary, however, one may simultaneously be a Jew and an atheist. Religion is only one element of Jewish ethnic identity, an identity that does not ultimately or completely depend on theological affirmation.

The ecclesiastical orientation, which is certainly not devoid of time and place components, nonetheless emphasizes allegiance to a set of ideas, theological or philosophical propositions, that exist independently of specific situation and circumstance. As the missionary outreach of the early church intensified, the Christian message was separated from the ethnic requirements of the Jewish people to stress the less tangible, more universal affirmations which would appeal to persons of any group or background. Ideas, later consolidated as creedal statements, are values without linkage to the basic space and time components of historical consciousness.

It is, then, in this instance suggested that self-definition as an *ethnos* is more likely to involve a consciousness of historical continuity than identity in the form of an *ecclesia* where history may actually be seen as an impediment.

Following WWI, Rabbi Mordecai Kaplan (1881–1983) began to develop a new movement in American Judaism called Reconstructionism. Naturalistic in philosophy, Reconstructionism held that Judaism is "an evolving civilization" of which religion is only one element. In describing Judaism as a civilization, Kaplan explicitly emphasized the ethnic dimension of Jewish identity. The movement he initiated has remained rather small, but its influence has been very widespread within Conservative and Reform Judaism and has become an integral part of the thinking of many rabbis and lay people in both of these Jewish streams.

A further consideration involves one's sense of personal past as a member of the group. Of particular interest is the concept, expressed in the Gospel of John (1:13; 3:3, 5) and repeated elsewhere in the New Testament (1 John 3:9; 4:7; 5:1, 4, 18; Gal 2:20; Cols 2:12; 2 Tim 2:11) that one should be "born of God." Joining the new church involved, not an ethnic allegiance, but an individual affirmation and communion with God through Jesus, the Christ. This perspective would be much more congenial to an evangelism that reached out to a wide variety of people, to groups with different backgrounds, practices, and traditions, some of which might be in conflict with other groups of potential new converts and which might have nothing in common with Jewish rituals. To reduce the importance assigned to historical factors might, then, actually enhance the attractiveness of the new faith. Second Corinthians 5:17 sets forth such a perspective: ". . . if anyone is in Christ, he is a new creation: the old has passed away, behold the new has come."

To be a Christian, to be "born of God" (or to be "reborn" as characterizes much contemporary Christian usage) involves the active reduction or even the obliteration of the past and the creation of an identity that is fundamentally existential and that focuses on present and future. Once the eternal salvation through Christ is proclaimed, once the climactic eschatological moment has occurred, history as we know it has come to an end, a new era has begun, and the believer exists on a theological plane that is independent of time and history. Individuals and groups that assign high value to futurity and declare that "the old has passed away" are unlikely to develop a significant interest in history. It is only a small step from "the past is but prologue" to "the past does not matter or need to exist at all."

For Jews, on the other hand, whose condition during the last two thousand years has been that of a minority in an often hostile environment, historical awareness functions to provide a sense of group identity, distinctiveness, and continuity. Through history, one learns of the experiences that differentiate one community from another and establish the nature of each group's uniqueness. To have been the object of medieval anti-Semitism, come from the *shtetl* region of Eastern Europe, descend from the likes of Maimonides and the Vilna Gaon and Moses Mendelssohn, and be linked to the early settlers of kibbutzim in Palestine—even if vicariously—such awareness forges connections and boundaries that depend on involvement with historical time and space.

A central demand of the Passover *Haggadah* is that "every Jew is obliged to think of himself/herself as though he/she were redeemed personally from Egypt." Jews may be unique among the world's groups to teach the art of "retrojection," of being able to cast one's self back through time and space to be a vicarious participant in past events at the same time as one maintains an objective sense of analytic distance. To be able to move back and forth through history means that a twenty-first-century Jew can also stand with Moses at Sinai, Amos at Beth El, Yochanan ben Zakkai at the Roman siege of Jerusalem, and every other personality, community, and event of the Jewish past. Retrojection makes it possible to bridge gaps between far-flung people and places, and to create a single, historical people, a common destiny, and a sense of mutual responsibility.

In Protestant Christianity, especially the Anglican and Episcopalian communions, there is significant attention to identification with the founders of Christianity, notably the apostles and some of the church fathers. This anchoring of contemporary Christianity in the early church's practices and faith, however, then skips the ensuing two thousand years. In the Lutheran liturgy, for example, one might expect reference to the Reformation and to Martin Luther, but except for a three-line, optional Collect in the back of the book, such mention is absent. As a Jew, I am surprised, even though I understand the existential nature of Christianity that emphasizes a personal, immediate, and uninterrupted relationship with Jesus as the Christ. Likewise, the English Book of Common Prayer talks about neither the Reformation nor the English Church, but devotes significant attention to the primitive or apostolic church.

This difference is highlighted in a comparison of the liturgies used by various denominations at regular, public worship. Scholars and professional clergy have access to specialized knowledge and insights that are generally not available to the laity. The prayer books, on the other hand, represent the distillate of what the group stands for. In an hour of worship, a member ought to be able to summarize what ideas and values are salient in the religion. A review of Christian materials leads to the inescapable conclusion that a consciousness of history is not one of the salient lessons the laity needs to grasp. The nearly invariable pattern is that Abraham had faith (as opposed to works), which was accounted to him as righteousness; Jesus lived, was crucified, and rose from the dead; and here we are in the twenty-first century. Intervening events and persons are not mentioned. Orthodox Jewish worship is conducted in Hebrew in the presence of congregants who often do not know what the words mean. But more liberal Jewish services strive for a balance of traditional forms and comprehension. In them, the historical focus is more apparent. Special holy days have been created to commemorate the Holocaust and to celebrate Israel, and there are occasional prayers that refer to historical personalities and events. The *Avodah* service on the afternoon of Yom Kippur annually rehearses the saga of Jewish history from creation to the hoped-for final redemption. A Jew at worship is frequently reminded that the past is important.

For Jews, this need to connect with other Jews, past and contemporary, is more critical than for Christians. Members of a majority group do not often need to think about the survival of their culture, and, therefore, can take their identity rather for granted. But, as a minority people beset by the cultural imperialism of host civilizations, Jews were compelled to strengthen the boundaries that denote their identity and limit the likelihood of assimilation. History, far more than theology, serves as an antidote to the disappearance of the Jewish community. The study of history played a psychological role for a people beset by uncertainty; it provided continuity and stability when the conditions of their daily lives often pointed in exactly the opposite direction. Particularly in the modern world, when shifts and flux appear as the only constants in everyday life, the unchanging nature of past reality may be something of an anchor and a comfort to people unsettled by the unceasing pressures of novelty and instability.

It may seem paradoxical, but it is relevant to conclude my thoughts about Jews and their fascination with history with some reference to the future. The Jewish notion of the messianic world-to-come is, nonetheless, still the world. The ideal future to which Jews look is not an obliteration of this world and all of the activities that occur in it or a recreation of a mythic world of the past. It constitutes an as-yet unrealized future time when human beings in partnership with God bring to fruition the values and ideals spoken about by the biblical prophets. History and human striving do not cease in the Jewish messianic future, but are characterized by the achievement of a paradise on earth and in time the likes of which we have only so far imagined in our highest aspirations.

A POSTSCRIPT

From everything that I have written so far about Jews and their involvement with history, one might be led to think that there is little that is problematic for me in this area. In the main, it is true that this sphere of thought has not been a particular tribulation for me. I am comfortable as a member of the Jewish people (despite my early upbringing that I have described earlier) and fascinated by our history. Part of what brought me to the rabbinate was a course in Jewish history that I took at Oberlin College in the fall of 1959. But that course only intensified and focused an interest in history that I had nurtured since childhood. Besides, I candidly admit that I have scant talent for mathematics, science, or music; but with history, I assimilate that kind of knowledge easily and quickly.

In these early years of the twenty-first century, there is some reason to believe that the dichotomous analysis that I have suggested is unraveling. Some mainstream Christian denominations have experimented on a church-by-church basis with the abandonment of fixed liturgies and their replacement with locally generated, ephemeral materials. This practice makes it possible to include in public worship references both to specific historical and contemporary events and personalities and the application of timeless doctrine to occurrences in time and place. It is too early to make any judgment about how popular or widespread this trend may become, but it does suggest the beginning of change in ecclesiastical attitudes toward history.

Among Jews, however, an opposite movement may be germinating—for a variety of reasons. As we have moved away from the immigrant experience, awareness of and interest in ethnicity among younger American

Jews has waned; there may be emerging a new definition of Jewish identity that moves closer to religious spirituality and belief than in the past. At the same time, we live in an age that has been widely characterized as ahistorical and even anti-historical. The pace of change in modern life is so rapid, especially in technological and scientific spheres, that what happened only a few years ago is often viewed as irrelevant. Why pay attention to yesterday when all that matters is tomorrow?

Finally, there is the issue of intermarriage, which has brought numerous new people into the Jewish community. These converts, however, *begin* their Jewish lives with no awareness of or connection or allegiance to the Jewish past. Even though efforts are made to help them acquire an ethnic consciousness, this may require a long period of learning and adjustment and may not be ultimately complete or successful. For them, Jewish identity will more likely be defined, at least for an extended transitional period, by theology or social ethics.

In our rapidly changing world, many sense that the only thing that is permanent is change. We see glimpses of the impact of this attitude in many American religious movements. Some denominations will respond reluctantly, even reject modernism; others will accept the challenge with greater or lesser degrees of enthusiasm. How this will play out in the future is yet to be seen. But we can reasonably expect that the intersection of historical consciousness and idea-based religiosity will appear differently in the future.

6

The Shape of Our Hope:
Messianic Dreams

IN MY PRE-TEEN YEARS, my parents were determined that my vocabulary would be devoid of unsavory four-letter words. To that end, they taught me the name of a Russian anarchist and intellectual, Prince Pyotr Alexeyevich Kropotkin. The prince's last name can be inflected in a variety of ways to express frustration, anger, confusion and even excitement and joy. For years, I said "Kropotkin" as a way of covering a multitude of linguistic options that would not have been acceptable in polite society.

I say this because, of course, there are four-letter words that we really should not use. On the other hand, there are four-letter words that are more than acceptable; they are desirable. Consider the word "love." No one could object to the voicing of that sentiment. Perhaps the most important four-letter word in the religious vocabulary, however, is the word "hope." More than anything, hope is a value that characterizes the religious quest and aspiration. As a rabbi, as a Jew, as a religious person, as a human being, the most meaningful thing that I can offer to another person is hope.

When we talk about hope in terms of the Jewish religious vision, we need to think about the way in which our tradition shapes time. Not every religious group thinks of time in the same way. Some, for example, hold up the ideal of a perfect past time and hope that the present will lead in circular fashion back to the days of that ancient glory. "If we could only be pure," they suggest, "like Adam and Eve in the garden of Eden, we would have fulfilled our hope." Perhaps others yearn for the pristine Christianity of the apostolic age before bureaucracy and politics allegedly corrupted the message of the emerging church. Others might hope for a return to the imagined piety of the Eastern European shtetl, or, if one is like Paul Gauguin, the beauty and simplicity of unspoiled Tahiti.

But a circular structuring of time is not the only way to think. Many people prefer to conceptualize time in a forward-looking mode. Their hope lies in an unrealized future rather than an idealized past. The hope for which they wish is not a paradise lost, but a paradise imagined, yet-to-be created. This notion of time is best described as linear rather than circular. Still others combine the two perspectives and think of time in a spiral modality, moving toward the future, but always influenced and conditioned by the past.

In most Jewish perceptions of hope, it is the linear version that dominates. The overwhelming tendency in the Jewish tradition is to believe that the world has never been perfect, that it certainly is not in our day and that the mission of the Jew is to serve as God's partner in the repair of the brokenness of our society. In Hebrew, this is called *Tikkun Olam*. In this regard—and here I revert to comments made earlier about the nature of God—it would appear that God in creation either determined not to create a perfect world or was unable to do so. Perhaps God deliberately left a sphere of unfinished business to give human beings a task of cosmic proportions, completing the work of creation, or perhaps perfection was never God's intention at the outset. The last verse in the first chapter of Genesis (1:31) reports that "God saw everything that He had made and, behold, it was very good." "Very good" is short of perfect; maybe perfection is reserved for God or for the messianic future.

In a book entitled *Souls on Fire*, Elie Wiesel quotes an adage from *Pirke Avot* (2:1): *Dah Mah L'ma'alah Mimchah*. In its original context, this meant that people should be aware of an all-seeing God who was above them, recording their deeds and preparing to judge them accordingly. But Weisel records that the early Hasidic master, the Maggid of Mezeritch, reinterpreted this saying to mean "that which is above you, namely, that which God will do, depends on you." The essence of what the Maggid taught—and which is in accord with most Jewish tradition—is that the burden of improving the condition of the world lies squarely on the shoulders of human beings. We cannot plead for divine assistance or intervention until we have done all that we are capable of doing. There is no escape from human responsibility or freedom; if we want a quasi-messianic future, it's largely up to us. A tennis analogy seems apt. God has initiated the game by serving Torah and decision-making potential into our court. Now, it is up to us to return serve by implementing godly values in our own lives and in the society around us. Of course, our return of serve is never going to be complete or perfect; we are, after all, only human and cannot, therefore, create a perfect or messianic world by ourselves. Only when we have done this and the ball is back on God's side of the net may we hope that God will continue the play and finish the messianic task. We can advance the process only so far; then, we need the help of the Almighty.

Extending the analysis that was begun in the essay on "history," we might ask ourselves: Is this indefinite, but heartily desired future primarily for the individual person or for society as a whole and for individuals only as they fit into that structure? It seems to me that this is not an either/or question, but one of priorities. Religions want to offer hope for the individual, but they also clearly want to proffer a vision of a better world. Some religions place one end of this continuum first; others prefer a different focus.

As an outsider, I observe that the Christian faith, based as it is on an ecclesiastical model, appears to begin with the individual and then moves to the larger society. The emphasis on absolution from original sinfulness is at the core of the Christian message, and that is an individual issue. Only someone who is reborn in Christ is enabled to be an agent for the propagation of Christian virtues into society at large. Judaism, on the other hand, takes the point of view that even fallible and imperfect human beings are commanded to implement divine values. There is a worldly and pragmatic dimension in Jewish thought that holds that even when one is not completely motivated or convinced, it is still vital to engage in the work of *Tikkun Olam*. One is reminded of the midrash of Nachshon ben Aminadav at the Reed Sea. The legend holds that the Israelites were fleeing the Egyptians, but they were forced to stop at the shore. They realized that the Egyptian forces were pursuing them, but they did not know how to proceed. Some began to pray; others formed committees to research possible solutions; still others panicked and wept. Meanwhile, Nachshon walked into the Sea. It was only because he moved forward in spite of uncertainty and then only when the water rose to his mouth did God cause a pathway to appear (*Mechilta beshallach*). The essence of the midrash is: Get busy now and ask questions and engage in debate later. If you don't like income taxes, pay them as required. Argue about the theoretical implications after April 15. If you don't want to slow down to 20 mph in a school zone, do it anyway. Your personal likes or dislikes are secondary to moving forward according to your obligations.

This interpretation of the Jewish messianic tradition impresses and attracts me because it places the major responsibility on human beings. It affirms human competency and potency, empowering people with the ability to make a world-changing difference. At the same time, it also admits that human endeavor alone cannot complete the task, that there are limits to human capability and that, while we can bring the world closer to its ideal state, unaided by God we cannot achieve the goal. Reasonable or realistic empowerment seems to me the right balance. It provides a purpose for human striving without opening the floodgates of self-aggrandizement or abandoning the posture of human humility.

A question that clergy are frequently asked is whether the messianic future will be ushered in by an individual messiah or whether it will be an impersonal era of perfection. We are also asked if this future time will be an extension of history and life as we know them today or if the world will be transformed into some kind of unearthly paradise. With reference to the latter query, the Jewish tradition generally suggests that the messianic era will occur within the confines of life as we presently experience it. The residents of that time will probably eat, drink, have sex and bear children, and very likely engage in gainful employment. In other words, the future era of perfection will be a linear extension of present-day existence, but under ideal conditions.

How does one know what to believe or anticipate? Jews have generally shied away from speculative theology, from guessing what will happen in areas where it seems impossible to gather evidence. There is a skeptical and rationalistic streak to the Jewish intellectual quest, and concern about the nature of the messiah and the messianic era plays a relatively minor role in Jewish thought and life. The tradition has devoted relatively scant attention to subjects where there could be no definitive answer, primarily for lack of evidence. How, after all, would one really know what happens after death or in the messianic future? We have no reports from the beyond, and there seems to be no methodology for finding out. So the consensus of rabbis and scholars of the past and of the present has been to skirt these questions and to focus, instead, on topics where there could be conclusive discussion. Thus, instead of inquiring about the nature of angels and how many of them could dance on the head of a pin, Jews centered their investigations on this-worldly questions. I may not know what life after death is all about, but I can tell you with relative clarity how to build a sukkah, when to say the *Shema* and how to identify an unethical or immoral act or person.

It is, perhaps, the best definition of Jewish faith to say that I shall concentrate my efforts on this life, on things, people and actions over which I have some control and then leave the speculative side of the equation to God. I shall try to live in such a way as to merit inclusion in the world to come, if such exists. But if there is nothing beyond the grave, I shall at least have had the satisfactions of living a good life, of doing what I believe God wants me to do and of making some kind of contribution to my fellow human beings.

Though it does not stem from a Jewish source, here one ought to be mindful of what is called "Pascal's Wager." Blaise Pascal (1623–1662) was a rationalistic French philosopher, mathematician, and physicist. He wanted to develop a way of persuading himself of the existence of God. In an elegant, but very simple proof that extended the science of probability and inaugurated the notion of decision-making theory, Pascal proposed a method that afforded him the maximal degree of comfort with theism short of absolute certitude. Because his proof still left some degree of uncertainty, Pascal declared that he was willing to bet the welfare of his eternal soul on his conclusion. Hence, it is termed his "Wager."[1] Though he was a Catholic, I find his reasoning persuasive and helpful; it has become a significant part of my religious vocabulary.

Some people ask: What motivates you to do the right thing if you do not anticipate either reward or punishment in the hereafter? I do not think in those terms, nor do I suspect that most Jews define their behavior because of future consequences. It is enough for me to have lived as good a life as I am able. The indefinite future is largely irrelevant, or in the immortal words of Rhett Butler, "Frankly, my dear, I don't give a damn!" In a somewhat more reverent phrasing, the rabbis taught (*Pirke Avot* 1:17) that "Intellectual inquiry is not the most important thing, but action." I'll leave the indefinite future in the sphere of God's judgment and action. My concept of faith translates as "trust." I'll do my part and then have faith or trust. Besides, if there is no afterlife, I'll never know the difference!

A frequent messianic question has to do with the historical character, Jesus of Nazareth. A recent poll from the Pew Research Center reports that as many a 34 percent of people who self-identified as Jews thought that Jesus could be the messiah.[2] If the future messiah is a single human being

1. See Pascal's *Pensées*, paragraph 233.

2. Laurie Goodstein, "Poll Shows Major Shift in Identity of U.S. Jews," *New York Times*, October 1, 2013.

(and not an impersonal era or age), then someone like Jesus could just as easily be that figure as anyone else. The jury is still out, however. Jews do not believe the messiah (in whatever form) has yet made an appearance. What is clear, from a Jewish perspective, is that the historical personality named Jesus could not have been the messiah. Why?

A great deal of the response has to do with expectations. From various biblical prophets, we garner ideas of what the ideal future might be like. It will be a time of peace and brotherhood, with lion lying down with lamb, with people beating their swords into plowshares. The ideal future world will be one of justice, mercy, and humility, if the prophet Micah (6:8) is right. Amos talks about justice and righteousness and about compassion and care for the less-fortunate. Isaiah tells us that Torah will go forth from Zion and the word of God from Jerusalem and that all the nations will acknowledge the sovereignty of the one God of Israel. A Davidic ruler will sit on a throne in Israel, ruling over an ingathering of Jews from the four corners of the world. People will sit under their vines and under their fig trees and no one shall make them afraid. Expectations like these, the core descriptions of an ideal future society, constituted and still frame the shape of the messianic anticipation of Jews.

In the first century CE, a Jew who was confronted with the claim that the messiah had appeared could consult this menu of expectations and ask a very straight-forward question: Have the predictions come to pass? Is the ideal world already upon us? Any reasonable observer at that time would have had to come to the conclusion that, quite to the contrary, the conditions of life in Judea under Roman domination were, if anything, worse than they had ever been. It was certainly not true that the prophetic image of the future world had come into reality and, QED, anyone who was proposed to be the messiah could not have qualified. Only when the conditions predicted by the prophets had come to pass could a messianic claimant be acknowledged as such. The notion of "the second coming of Christ" deals with frustrated expectations by asserting that they will only be realized when Jesus returns. Meanwhile, Jews are still waiting for the first and only coming.

As Christianity developed, additional considerations led Jews to reject the messianic identity assigned to Jesus. The primary evangelical outreach of the early Church was into the Graeco-Roman Empire, where the philosophy of Neoplatonism held sway among the opinion makers of the culture. The Neoplatonic concept of God was very different from the God of the Hebrew Scriptures. The latter was a God of involvement with the world and its residents, a God who reacted and acted, a God who spoke and heard and moved. The God of the philosophers, however, was the "unmoved and unmoving mover," the static source of all other motion in the cosmos. Such a God could not, however, be responsive to human needs. To harmonize the two concepts of God, Christianity identified Jesus with the Active Intellect (*Logos* in the opening verses of the Gospel according to John), the power that translates the purely intellectual dimension of the distant God into action in the terrestrial sphere. As a device to harmonize the biblical and Greek systems, this works.

The center of gravity of the Jewish world, however, left Judea and after a brief sojourn in the Galilee, moved eastward into the Mesopotamian valleys. But Greek thought had not become influential in this region. The biblical conception of God retained its potency and reality in this environment, so there was little motivation to accommodate to Neoplatonism among the rabbinic opinion makers, and the solution adopted by Christianity seemed unnecessary. The role that Jesus played as an intermediary between the world of matter and the world of pure intellect was superfluous; Jews could still approach God directly and could anticipate the same kinds of responses that they had received in the Scriptures.

There are other reasons why Jews have not considered Jesus as the messiah. Here are several. The New Testament reports that Jesus performed miracles and that those acts confirmed his messianic status. Two of the most renowned of these feats involved reviving Lazarus after he had died (John 11) and feeding the multitude on fish and bread (Matt 15 and elsewhere). These are, indeed, remarkable acts, but they are not unique. In 2 Kings 4, the prophet Elisha brings a dead child back to life by breathing into his mouth (an early account of CPR) and helps a poor woman by causing her supply of oil to multiply exponentially. Elisha lived approximately eight hundred years before Jesus. If this kind of miracle supports one's claim to the messianic title, one might assert that temporal precedence alone should give priority to Elisha.

An additional consideration regards the differing anthropologies of Christianity and Judaism. Interpreting the expulsion of Eve and Adam from the Garden (Gen 3), the early framers of Christian doctrine determined that this meant a change from the "very good" in Genesis' first chapter to sinful and tainted. The fall from divine grace could not be reversed by human agency because whatever actions people might take to regain God's favor would inevitably be impure. Their source was an impure human being, so their salvific quality was impaired. The only way to return humans to divine grace was through the intervention of a person or a power that did not partake of the original corruption of the species. Since original sinfulness, like all other essential human characteristics, is believed to be transmitted from one generation to the next by means of sexual reproduction, the agent of redemption had to be generated by immaculate or asexual conception. In the Christian theological scheme, then, Jesus, the only person born free of sin, is able to be the vehicle for the removal of the taint of original sinfulness.

Jews understand the expulsion from Eden differently. We accept the reality that impulses for both good and evil compete within every human being and believe that the essence of the human quest is to make ethical and moral choices between these two forces. We think of sin as a specific act that offends against ourselves, other individuals, society, or God. But we reject the notion that there was a fundamental change in the character of the human person at the eastern gate of Eden. Simply put, since we do not acknowledge the same anthropological change that occasions the need for Jesus in Christianity, we have no religious or personal need for him as the messiah.

As the new faith developed into the fourth century, the nature of the Trinity was hotly debated among Christians. While they came to some resolution on the question of the relationship of its three constituent elements, Jews never understood how one and three are the same. Raised on the absolute monotheism of the *Shema*, Jews found the notion of trinitarianism confusing and unacceptable. I asked about this one day when I was playing golf with one of my good friends, Msgr. Seamus McGowan, a gentle and lovely Irish priest. He looked at me with a twinkle in his eye and in his inimitable brogue said: "Ken, it's a mystery, a sacred mystery." He had neatly summarized the core commitment of his faith, but it could not suffice for me or for most Jews. We do not side with Tertullian, the early church father, who wrote that he believed in the resurrection precisely because it was impossible (*credo quia impossible*). For a rationalist, such as myself, such faith is what is impossible.

Finally, through it is painful, one must mention the history of Christian anti-Jewish persecution. From John of Chrysostom to Visigothic legislation to crusades and inquisition, to Russian pogroms and even to the Nazi claim that *Gott mit uns* (God is with us), what has been perpetrated in the name of the Prince of Peace hardly evokes admiration. And though any fair observer must acknowledge that America in the twenty-first century is different than most earlier times and that contemporary Christians are worlds apart from those who terrorized Jewish communities of past eras, it is still hard to shake free from all the negative associations. For all of the positive meanings that the cross has for Christians, it is difficult for a Jew who is aware of this history to look at this symbol without a shudder of both past and present recognition. Interfaith relations are undoubtedly at their best level ever. Various surveys show conclusively that American anti-Semitism has declined from a pre-WWII level of 50 percent who declared that they did not like Jews to just under 20 percent, perhaps even as low as 9 percent. That is a substantial and welcome change, but 20 percent on the American population nonetheless translates into roughly sixty million people who harbor negative feelings and images about Jews. A good number of these fellow citizens likely profess the Christian faith. We've come a long way; we still have a ways to go.

When people are in need of hope, they are often emotionally vulnerable. This state of mind leaves them open to manipulation and potential abuse. Grieving families can be persuaded to make excessive financial commitments by unscrupulous funeral directors; fragile women may be sexually assaulted by counselors who are prepared to take advantage of them; unsettled teenagers can be targets for peers who ply them with drugs, alcohol and sex. Every clergy person has known of examples of this kind of coercion. In the realm of messianic speculation, too, con artists and charlatans are only too eager to engage in similar predation.

Religious history of all denominations is replete with characters who have claimed messianic status (or about whom that status was alleged). Invariably, these remarkable and charismatic personalities turned out to be false messiahs.

In the seventeenth century, the growing interest in Jewish mysticism (*Kabbalah*) that had begun among émigrés from Iberia who had moved to Turkey and to the area of Tiberias in the Galilee led to a period of messianic fervor. The outburst of enthusiasm was stoked by a singular person, a man named Shabbetai Zevi (1626–1676) who lived his entire life in Turkey. Zevi claimed to be the messiah, with such success that a large part of European Jewry sold their property and goods and prepared to join him upon his proposed triumphal entry into Jerusalem. Unfortunately, the Sultan took a dim view of this pretender who possessed such disruptive potential. He offered Zevi a proposition: convert to Islam or die. Courageously, Shabbetai Zevi converted, telling his followers that the messiah sometimes has to do inexplicable things. His following largely evaporated in the wake of this apostasy, but Shabbetaians continued well into the nineteenth and even twentieth centuries.

A century later, a German messianic pretender arose. Jacob Frank (1726–1791) led a smaller, but not inconsequential movement known eponymously as the Frankists. His premise was that the messianic time could not begin until the corrupt world had disappeared and was replaced by a new world of purity. To help the old order self-destruct, Frank espoused a theory of purification through transgression. He volunteered to lead Jewish society on a downward plunge into degradation by engaging in all sorts of dissolute misbehavior and corrupt acts. I must admit a certain admiration and fascination with Jacob Frank. Even if he was a totally fraudulent messianic pretender, to pose as the ringleader of sin to help the world save itself constitutes a level of audacity and *chutzpah* that must evoke a gasp of fascination.

From a Jewish perspective, the history of messianic pretension has invariably been followed by unrealized expectation. But that record does not eliminate the striving and the goal. Jewish life is incurably optimistic and hopeful concerning the future. The world will be a better place tomorrow, and we shall be among those who are agents of such improvement. And if the messianic future does not occur within our days, then at least we shall have the satisfaction of knowing that we were among those who strove to push our society closer to the desired end. As we have learned in *Pirke Avot* 2:16: "It is not incumbent upon you to complete the work. But you are not free to desist from it."

7

It's Not Supposed to Be Like This: The Problem of Theodicy

THE PROBLEM OF HOW does a Jew pray when the God who is supposed to answer prayers did not respond at Auschwitz is the most vexing contemporary theological dilemma. But the most enduring challenge to faith is the question "why do bad things happen to good people?" The query originated when the first human being said "It's not supposed to be like this," and it has continued in uninterrupted fashion through the ages, in virtually all cultures and societies, down to our own time.

The root of the problem for Jews (and for other people who take the Torah seriously) is what Moses said in the name of God in the twenty-eighth chapter of the book of Deuteronomy. In this very long oration, Moses lays out the paradigmatic understanding of divine justice. He tells the assembled Israelites that there will be a one-to-one correlation of behavior and consequences. In the first fourteen verses, he puts forward the proposition that, if you follow God's commandments and do the right thing, then good things will come to you. Righteous behavior leads, inevitably so it seems, to positive outcomes. On the other hand, the ensuing fifty-three verses describe the negatives that will result from misbehavior and unfaithfulness. Even the most cursory reading of this enumeration of curses ought to lead the lector to the conclusion that this is not a path one would ever want to follow. And then the chapter concludes with verse 69 that makes very clear that this syllogism of automatic, mechanical reward and punishment is indisputably underwritten by the divine authority: "These are the words of the covenant which the Lord commanded Moses to make with the children of Israel in the land of Moab, beside the covenant which He made with them in Horeb."

The Torah, traditional Jews have always believed, is the infallible word of God, revealed at Sinai, transmitted without error through all the generations. God neither makes mistakes nor lies nor deceives, so these words must be true and accurate. But wait a moment. How is it, if the Torah's promises are correct, that things keep happening in our lives that prompt us to reiterate the refrain "It's not supposed to be like this"? Bad things continue to happen in the lives of decent and righteous people, and often enough scoundrels reap rewards that according to Deuteronomy should not be theirs. The fate of individuals, peoples, even nations hardly seems to correspond with God's promises and the expectations we have developed as a result of them. Somehow, there is a disjunct between action and result, between behavior and consequence. Yet we like to live in a world that makes sense, so we try to understand this situation and explain the failures of divine justice in ways that might alleviate our sense of alienation from the original divine guarantee.

To summarize at the very beginning of this discussion (which will almost entirely be conducted within a Jewish frame of reference), the tradition has proposed a variety of solutions to the quandary, all of which have partial validity and none of which is free from challenge. In short, no one has yet come up with an explanation that is so comprehensive and satisfying that it is invulnerable from attack. So the problem persists, and people continue to wrestle with it. We call it *theodicy*, a word that comes from two Greek words meaning "God" and "justice." But when we refer to the problem of theodicy, we are virtually always referring to the discontinuity between the ideal spelled out in Deuteronomy and the reality that we experience in our daily lives. It's the apparent miscarriage of divine justice that we are always trying to understand and explain.

One way to handle this failure of reality to match the expectations of the ideal is to attribute the problem to the operation of a fundamental source of pure evil in the cosmos. Because we humans cannot deal easily with abstractions—and a "source of evil" is an abstraction—we have come to personify this evil force. In Hebrew tradition, it is called *Satan*, which in context means the accusing angel or God's prosecuting attorney. In Islamic lore, this same entity is named *Shaitan*. Nearly every folk culture has its devil figure, its ogre, its malevolent personality. In dualistic traditions, like Persian Zoroastrianism, it is the negative side of existence, often depicted in blackish color, and in Jewish mysticism (which verges on dualism) it is called *Sitra Achra*, the other side. Cultures and their religions have found it convenient to explain evil as the effect of this malicious force; "It was the Devil who caused bad things to happen."

For a monotheist, however—and this obviously include Jews—this analysis is in conflict with the basic belief in the oneness of God. A source of power and authority cannot exist independent of the unitary God. So, in the biblical book of Job, Satan comes before God and requests permission to try the protagonist's faith. He has no right to do so without first acknowledging his subservience to his divine overlord, and it is only once God agrees to Job's trial that Satan has permission to proceed. The biblical book is almost entirely the account of misfortunes that rain down upon Job and his reaction to them. Even though he is convinced that the fate that has come upon him is undeserved, at least in its severity, he is unwavering in his faith that God is just. When he seeks an explanation from the Almighty, he is rebuffed in a magnificent extended poetic answer that declares that God is in charge and that, as a human being, Job can never understand God's activity or reasons. As I read the last chapter of the book (42), the narrative ends when Job submits to the inscrutable God and "God accepted Job" (42:9). The remaining five verses (42:10-14) are a happy ending that simply undercuts the basic contention of the book: God and man are altogether different and the only way to gain divine favor, even in spite of a satanic attempt to undermine one's faith, is to accept without question the sovereignty of God. When God restores Job and then doubles his fortune (42:10), I react by declaring that this cannot be by the same author who wrote most of the book; it sounds phony, as if the author of this appendix could not bear the militant agnosticism with which the "real" Job is left only a few verses earlier.

In any event, one might want to react to God's approval of Satan's plan in two ways. First, God does not need to approve. Job is presented as a righteous, pious, and God-fearing man. Is this not enough? Or, is God so fragile of ego and lacking in psychic security that he must have this extraordinary proof of Job's fealty? If one looks at Job's trial from the vantage of the human sufferer, what kind of a mean and vicious God would inflict such miseries on a good man, just to prove what is already known of a certainty. The book of Job presents God in a much-less-than favorable light, even if the poetry is exalted. A thoroughgoing monotheist who proposes Satan as the source of terrestrial evil can do so only by adopting one of two choices. Either Satan is independent of God's supervision, in which case monotheism is no longer viable. Or, Satan's power comes directly from God, in which case God is ultimately responsible for the evils of the world. Neither one of these options is especially palatable. The unacceptable nature of both of these options helps us understand why this explanation of why divine justice appears to run amiss and cannot satisfy the needs of one who looks for a wholesome explanation.

The notion that God tests human beings has a venerable biblical root. In Genesis 22, Abraham is told to take Isaac to Mount Moriah and sacrifice him there. God is apparently interested to see if the patriarch's faith and obedience are strong enough to survive the ordeal. When God is assured of Abraham's loyalty ("... now I know that you fear God, seeing that you have not withheld your son, your only son, from Me," 22:12b), God relents, substitutes a ram and blesses Abraham. During the later rabbinic period (after 70 CE), the idea that God tests people's fidelity came to be known as *Yissurin shel Ahavah*, chastisements prompted by divine love. These sufferings were inflicted, so the theory goes, because God loves the Jews, knows that they can bear up under the stress of persecution and oppression, and that they will consequently accrue even greater reward in the world to come. As I indicated at the outset of this discussion, this explanation, no less than the notion of the Devil, cannot be allowed to persist without challenge. Could not, one is compelled to ask, an omnipotent and benevolent God (and these are, after all, attributes accepted by both medieval and modern traditional Jews) construct a reward system that does not involve the severe affliction of a people with whom that God is in loving covenant? Would not the recompense of a good and godly life free of chastisements be sufficient? Is it, perhaps, that God is not able to eliminate the misfortunes faced by Jews in the real world, but that the victims themselves have found a way to rationalize the evils that beset them? Or, even worse, that the omnipotent God is not so benevolent as previously imagined and that, therefore, the ills that befall us are not only tokens of divine favor, but equally indications that God has a sadistic streak as one of the divine attributes? Whatever the objection, the concept that God brings chastisements upon the Chosen People out of love is a hard pill to swallow.

I stood in the elevator in the clinical building of the Mayo Clinic in Rochester, MN. An obviously Muslim father and mother were wheeling their seriously ill daughter to a doctor's examination room. As they reached their floor, I quietly said to the father: "I hope she gets better. *Insh Allah.*" May it be God's will. He responded: *Shukhran*, thank you, and they left the elevator. The idea that what happens on earth is God's will is connected to the idea of the Devil because, at least in a monotheistic religion, both assert that all actions ultimately derive from divine volition. If "it isn't supposed to be like this," if bad things happen to people who appear to deserve a better fate, this concept holds that whatever befalls us comes from God, even the negatives. Of course, in our daily lives we tend toward an inconsistent application of this premise. We like to take personal responsibility for the good things that happen—I studied hard and am responsible for the good grade on my history exam; I worked diligently, so I get credit for the promotion. But when unpleasantness rears its head—when a young adult dies, when the physics test comes back with a failing grade—the common tendency is for the aggrieved person to exclaim "Why did God do this to me?" Unfortunately, the theory doesn't work this way. If the bad occurrences are caused by God, then so must it be with the good; you cannot affirm only one pole of the equation. It's all or nothing.

I know that people often ascribe positive outcomes in some way to divine influence. It is certainly possible that we are motivated and strengthened by our belief in God's powers, that we use them to enhance our own abilities and potencies. But this is a far cry from the acceptance of a fulsome determinism or fatalism. To ascribe everything to "the will of God" is to remove actions entirely from the sphere of human responsibility and influence. On the other hand, to say that God and God's teachings have influenced me to make better choices or to take better advantage of help and strength when they are presented to me still leaves the basic responsibility and accountability in the human sphere. And that is how we actually live our lives.

Several decades ago, a young teenage boy in Miami watched a particularly gruesome and savage show on his home television. He then left his house and replicated the ghastly murder he had seen. When he was brought to trial, his defense was that he was under external compulsion; the TV show had forced him to action, so the fault could not be his. Not surprisingly, the judge dismissed this line of reasoning and maintained that our society and the individuals who live within it cannot escape personal culpability for their shortcomings. The idea of casting the blame for the untoward events in our lives on "the will of God" exempts us from responsibility, and that flaw alone makes it an unsatisfactory response to the problem of theodicy. It shares in the same problem one might have with the idea of the Devil because it makes God the root of all evil. And if this is God's role, then why would one want to associate with a God who causes infant crib deaths, disease of every sort, or pathological and sociopathic behavior? If God is behind social aberrations, premature deaths of innocent children, and illicit acts, frankly I would not be a rabbi, and I would probably never set foot in a religious edifice. So, I am among the multitude who might piously say "May it be God's will," but without meaning that there is some kind of a direct chain of causation between divine intention and result. It just doesn't work that way for me or for most people, so the idea of divine determinism won't adequately explain why "it's not supposed to be like this."

It is likely that the most common way of dealing with the perception that events on earth do not correspond to the expectations of divine justice is to assert that there is a life after death when an audit of each person's life will rectify any errors in the terrestrial ledger. Thus, the dominant image of Yom Kippur relates to a final day of judgment when a book of accounts is opened for ten days in heaven and the fate of each person is inscribed. The prayer *Unetaneh Tokef* makes clear that each individual's destiny is decreed and sealed during those days of awe. It is a comforting thought for many people that, even if this present life is unfair and difficult, the great Judge of the universe will straighten out the book of each person's life in the hereafter.

This concept notwithstanding, the Jewish view of afterlife finds very little support in the Hebrew Scriptures. There are people who have already committed to a belief in life after death and who then read that belief back into the biblical text. Thus, one may find an interpreter who say that the phrase "gathered to his people" (as in Gen 25:8 and 17, 35:29, 49:33; Deut 32:50 and elsewhere) means that the authors of the Bible had a defined notion of the hereafter. A more common understanding of this phrase is "he died and was buried with his ancestors"; most commentators would not consider this a clear statement regarding existence after death. There may be a few allusions to the hereafter in late biblical literature (Dan 12:2, for one example), but the consensus of scholars is that the Hebrew Bible does not offer us any significant guidance about what happens after we die. The great medieval philosopher, Saadia Gaon (Babylonia, tenth century) wrote that the promises of rewards and punishments outlined in Deuteronomy applied to this world only (*Book of Beliefs and Opinions* 9:2).

A full-blown concept of life after death was the creation of the Pharisees, beginning in the first pre-Christian century. The Sadducees rejected this idea, since they found no explicit mention of it in the Bible (and especially in the Torah), but the Pharisees innovated such a belief as a way to deal with the injustices and unfair aspects of life under Roman domination. From the Pharisees, the theology spread into patristic Christianity and then into both medieval Christian and Jewish thought. In the Jewish realm, there is no dogmatic statement regarding this subject and, therefore, a great deal of individual variation among rabbis and communities. For Maimonides, it was an article of faith to which a pious Jew would naturally assent, but not a proposition that was susceptible to philosophic or theological proof. In the modern Jewish world, the basic stance of most people is that we have no way of knowing what will happen after we die; there is no methodology that is verifiable enough to convince us. That a concept of life after death is not subject to scientific verification does not make it any the less true, but its claim to truth is of a different nature than a claim within the scientific sphere of inquiry. In any event, what a Jew may or may not believe about life after death is entirely optional and open.

What is equally important to note is that this idea is not a way to make sense of apparent miscarriages of divine justice in the life of any individual or group. Other schemes may attempt that kind of explanation (although not adequately or convincingly), but the idea of the hereafter does not. Rather, instead of explaining why the events happened, it seeks to respond by realigning the consequences of the events more in keeping with normative expectations.

If God is not responsible for the ills that afflict us, particularly when they do not seem to be appropriate responses to our behavior, then perhaps we ought to turn toward the other end of the continuum. Deuteronomy, after all, states that the curses that befall us are occasioned by our own misdeeds and infidelities. The Hebrew term for this idea is *mip'nei chatoteinu*, "on account of our own sins." Even if we think our misfortunes are undeserved, we are deluding ourselves by maintaining the pretense of our own goodness. This is the position Job's three friends adopted in the biblical book: "You must have done something terrible, because catastrophic maladies like these are never happenstance; they are always the legitimate response to and consequence of our own failings." Job steadfastly asserts that he is not perfect, but that he has not done anything so bad as to have deserved the disaster that has occurred in his life. As we observers already know, what happened to Job was part of a divine test, but the protagonist is left without explanation. His real fate is to be saddled with a radical agnosticism; he persists in his faith without any knowledge of why his life crumbled into ruins.

There are Jews today who continue to believe in the theory of *mip'nei chatoteinu* because it does explain why life does not turn out as we expect. Unfortunately, the syllogism works in a reverse fashion—from consequence to cause. If a bad thing happens, then it is incumbent on the person who accepts this rationale to find a suitable reason (read: sin sufficient to justify the consequence). In a book entitled *The Amen Response* by Shalom Y. Gross, we read that (if people say *amen*) "with the fullest of concentration . . . their decree of seventy years [will be] torn up and given more years of life."[1] Saying this one word properly and loudly, the author asserts, removes all evil decrees. But failure to say *amen* with full intentionality can result in all sorts of untoward and undesirable results.[2] In another book that I have unfortunately misplaced, I once read that the Shoah occurred because Jews all over the world failed to light their Sabbath candles in the prescribed manner. The hyperbolic nature of these claims is so outrageous as to render them risible—if they were not simultaneously so obscene in their implications.

The concept of *mip'nei chatoteinu* is, at least to my way of thinking, a method of holding the victim accountable for his/her own misfortunes. It is doubtlessly true that we bring some of our problems upon ourselves. The seriously diabetic adult who insists on eating sugary foods and then suffers an amputation has mostly himself to blame. Others who persist in self-destructive habits cannot escape responsibility for the hurtful and unpleasant consequences. To that extent, the theory works. But for calamities that come upon the apparently innocent, to assert that the victim is the cause of his/her own downfall pushes the envelope of unethical and immoral thinking beyond the bounds of the acceptable. In no case is this more obvious than in the case of the 1,500,000 young Jewish children who were murdered during the Shoah. It's altogether impossible to believe that they died because of their own sins—most were too young to have sinned in any grievous way—and even more unacceptable to think that the guilt of their elders descended upon them and led to their martyrdom. The flaws that arise from the notion of *mip'nei chatoteinu* are simply so severe as to disqualify this concept as an acceptable rationale for many forms of human suffering.

If explanations of why "It's not supposed to be like this" based on divine intentionality and/or human sinfulness do not satisfy, then perhaps we ought

1. Shalom Y. Gross, *The Amen Response* (New York: Mosad Brucha Tova, 1981), n.p.

2. http://www.chabad.org/library/article_cdo/aid/261102/jewish/The-Laws-of-Responding-Amen.htm.

to turn our attention to the nature of God. In the chapter that dealt with God, we approached the idea of a limited God. This idea that gained popularity through the writings of Alfred North Whitehead, Charles Hartshorne, John B. Cobb, and Pierre Teilhard de Chardin, along with many others, proposes a God that is in a constant process of development, even as both the physical and human worlds are ever growing and changing. It may be wrong, then, to expect such a developing God either to intend or be able to intervene to prevent unexpected and undesirable events from occurring. This is what Harold S. Kushner proposes in this book, *When Bad Things Happen to Good People*. God cannot or will not intervene, but reacts in parallel with human reactions by suffering and comforting those who are afflicted. We are now closer to some explanation of so-called undeserved suffering; at least we know it happens because God cannot prevent it. But that leaves open the penetrating question: If God cannot intervene or wills not to intervene, of what utility is there to such a deity? Can we not proceed in our lives, supporting and comforting each other in the face of affliction, but without the additional encumbrance of a deity who is fundamentally impotent?

A second proposal in much the same direction posits that the Creator God deliberately withdrew from the arena of human activity and left us to our own devices. What seems important is to assess the reason for this divine departure. One can hold the concept of *deus absconditus* simply by asserting that God's role was to create the universe, to set the process in motion and then to leave. This is the fundamental premise of Enlightenment-era deism, and there are many people who find it an acceptable explanation of why the world does not accord with the deuteronomic notion of invariable divine fairness and justice. This theory, too, works unless one asks whether there is any use for a divine presence or reason even to assert the existence of such an absent God.

Each of these proposed explanations of the problem of theodicy has some cogency and attraction. Yet no one of them—or even a combination of some of them—is so compelling as to be entirely satisfying and persuasive. One might be tempted in the face of this dilemma, a situation that has engaged the very best religious thinkers over the millennia, to declare that the universe is entirely absurd and chaotic. There are no explanations and no rationales; life just happens and sometimes it brings joy and happiness, while at other times we are forced to confront despair, ugliness, and defeat. Too bad! That's the way it is; that's all there is; there is nothing more. You don't have any choice except to confront with brutal realism whatever fate comes your way and cope with it as best you can. If there is a power greater than humans, it has no influence on what happens to us because our lives are altogether unpredictable and irrational.

The nihilism of such an approach seems to me just as unsatisfactory as all the other ways of thinking about theodicy. None of us wants to live in a universe that is entirely devoid of rationality and order. Maybe it's just pious wish-fulfillment, but a chaotic cosmos simply does not appeal to most people. Fortunately, there are some other thoughts that bear on the issue.

At the end of the first chapter of Genesis, the biblical text tells us that "God saw everything that had been created and, behold, it was very good" (1:31). "Very good" is short of "perfect." They are far from the same thing. It leaves room for both physical and behavioral fallibility. Our bodies are imperfect and human, and sometimes they fall victim to the weaknesses and the frailties of the flesh. While the ideal lifespan predicted by the psalmist is seventy or even eighty years (90:10), our less-than-perfect physical selves do not always abide by the average expectation; some live longer, but some become ill or die far short of the goal. Such is the way of all flesh. In more ways than the span of our lives, the Creator judged that we should be limited: our mental power, our reach, our financial resources, even our goodness. All of these are finite by the decision that we should be human and not God. The corollary of this understanding, however, is that imperfection is built into the essence of the universe and human life by divine design. We may have been created "little lower than the angels" (Ps 8:6), but the sometimes bitter truth is that we are always lower. If untoward and unexpected events happen in our lives, it is because that is the way we were created; they are consequences of our humanness.

But one can also look at being human from a much more positive perspective. If God withdrew deliberately after creation or after the revelation of the covenant at Sinai, we might understand that distancing as a way to leave room for human endeavor. One is reminded of the Kabbalistic notion of *shevirat ha-keilim*, the breaking of the primordial vessels of the universe. According to this mythic interpretation, the original creation resembled a series of crystalline spheres, each embedded within the next largest. When God withdrew, a vacuum was formed, and the ensuing decrease in pressure caused the fragile spheres to implode. Shattered fragments of the spheres, now identified as the essence of evil, floated through space in disarray. It became the role of human beings to serve as God's partners in the process of *tikkun olam*, the repair of the broken world. Our mission is to assist God by restoring the original integrity of the spheres, at least to the extent that human beings can perform this task, but equally to recognize that, so long as the crystal fragments remain unrestored, evil and imperfection must be part of our worldly lives. At one and the same time, the Kabbalistic myth succeeds in explaining the persistence of evil and the exalted nature of the human role as God's covenant partner.

To adopt the notion that human beings are (or can be) God's allies in the restoration of a shattered world automatically implies a rejection of determinism. If the human role is to have any real meaning, then our acts must be the result of the freedom to choose. Human actions performed under compulsion from some outside force are no longer free human actions but the results of duress and coercion. We must be free to choose the good and the right, but we also cannot negate the possibility that we might choose badly and, either directly or indirectly, occasion undesirable consequences. Bad things will also happen simply by virtue of the persistent imperfections of the unreconstructed world. Until the world is restored to its original pristine state by a combination of human and divine actions, we should never be surprised if "it's not the way it's supposed to be."

I want to say one more thing about this issue before turning to what one might consider the core question. The problem of theodicy is usually phrased in terms of God's failure to act fairly and justly. God, it is asserted based on texts such as those in Deuteronomy, has elaborated a structure of equity in the treatment of human behavior. If you act righteously, a reward will ensue; but if you misbehave, then just as surely punishment will follow. When that paradigm doesn't seem to work, the tendency is to blame the author of the system for failing to keep the promise. We might, however, want to look at the issue from the other end of the spectrum. In South Texas, we sometimes sing a Mexican song (or Spanish or Tex-Mex, depending on your predilection): "ai, ai, ai, ai . . ." Perhaps the problem lies not with God, but with the "I," with the individual human being whose expectations have been frustrated and who, because he/she cannot accept that the frailty of the flesh, the consequences of prior bad judgments or the unknowability of any divine plan or purpose, turns a virulent accusation to a source outside him/herself. Projection is a powerful psychological device, but it no more solves the problem of theodicy than all the more elaborate theories. It represents an unhealthy displacement of responsibility and a deflection of effective coping mechanisms. Truth to tell, the only realistic strategy is to admit that something terrible has happened in my life. It doesn't have any clear rationale or explanation. What I need to do is recognize that I am faced with a choice: I can wallow in grief, become the victim of my anger and remain a bitter, sullen, and unhappy person, or I can choose to accept the unfortunate event and then make the best of the future of my life. If I elect the former course, when I come upon good things in the future, I turn aside and reject them. Alternatively, if goodness and happiness and love are ahead of me, without forgetting the sadness of the past, I can embrace them actively and move forward to a satisfying and meaningful life.

There is a Conservative Jewish congregation in Buenos Aires, Argentina that bears what I consider to be the best name for a synagogue in the entire world. It was founded on May 3, 1944 by Jews who had fled Nazi Europe just before the outbreak of the Second World War. They were committed to the proposition that Jewish life could and should continue and so they called their new synagogue *Lamrot Hakol*, "In Spite of Everything." That they could assert this conviction in the face of the catastrophic destruction of European Jewry and even of their own families offers us a model of how to deal with the tragic occurrences that occasionally darken our own lives.

Having said all this about the philosophical dimensions of the theodicy issue, we ought still to ask a fundamental question from the perspective of the practicing clergy. Is this a theological/philosophical problem, or is it really a pastoral problem? For someone like myself, who has spent over five decades in the active rabbinate it is the rare month when the "practical" issue of theodicy does not arise. We sit in the office or at someone's home and weep together. Someone quite young is afflicted with a terminal disease. A terrible automobile accident leaves a young adult permanently disabled. A troubled person commits suicide. Death occurs when, by all rights and expectations, the person should have lived many more years. During the nearly ten years that I was the Rabbi of Temple Beth El in Madison, WI, I had the unwelcome duty of officiating at the burial of fifteen children under the age of three. That's one and a half such deaths per year, a record I would gladly have relinquished at every moment. In not one of these and other cases have the survivors ever asked for a rational, theological, or philosophical discussion. The real and only effective solution to the dilemma of theodicy is caring and support, love, kindness, and intimacy. In abstract terms, they may feel (often only temporarily) abandoned by God. But if people who are committed to the values of God express them through silent compassion and insistent involvement, the first steps toward recovery and a return to a rich and full life have been taken. There may be moments in the months to come for a more rational analysis, but the most positive remedy is an outpouring of love and support for the embittered person. It doesn't always work, but the best medicine is still a strong and prolonged hug.

8

It's a Different World: Anti-Semitism and America

ANY JEW WHO KNOWS the history of his or her people is aware that anti-Jewish sentiments and actions very much predate the emergence of Christianity. The book of Exodus tells of the enslavement of the Israelites, usually dated roughly in the early Hyksos period (ca. 1600 BCE). The book of Esther recounts a somewhat later episode in which King Ahashuerus and his prime minister, Haman, proposed to exterminate the Jews of Persia because they would not conform to the king's laws and because Haman sought to expropriate their property. Seleucids, under Antiochus Epiphanes IV, sought to convert the Temple in Jerusalem to an idolatrous altar, and in the third pre-Christian century an Egyptian priest named Manetho disseminated virulently anti-Jewish propaganda. This kind of Judeophobia was based very little on religious principle and derived most of its energy from the power ambitions of imperial regimes.

As a general principle, I suggest that anti-Jewish manifestations are largely the result of economic and social power conflicts. When such confrontations were salient, Jews suffered; when they were quiescent, Jews fared far better. Thus, for example, in early Muslim Spain (approximately 900–1200), Jews experienced a golden age during which they reached high positions in the government and the military and attained a good measure of economic prosperity. Literature, music, scientific endeavors, and traditional Jewish textual inquiry flourished. Beginning about 1215, their fortunes began to decline as Muslims developed the administrative and managerial skills necessary to govern southern Spain. Jews were no longer needed; their diminished value led to anti-Jewish manifestations and legislation. In northern Spain, however, the Catholic Reconquista was able to take advantage of Jewish abilities in its earliest phase. By the early fourteenth century, however, Jews could be replaced by competent Christian bureaucrats, and so the process of marginalization resumed. By the early fifteenth century, Catholic authorities were importuning the king further to demean the Jewish community, and it was not long until Tomas de Torquemada convinced Ferdinand and Isabella that their realm would be more stable and godly if all of its residents were devotees of a single faith. The last Muslims were driven across the Straits of Gibraltar in 1492, making Andalucia an exclusively Christian region, and the Jews of the entire kingdom were given the option in the same year either to convert or to leave in the month of August.

So what role does religion play if my contention that secular factors are largely to blame for anti-Jewish statements and actions? We certainly know that early in the history of the Christian church, various leaders expressed highly negative views of Jews. The Gospel according to St. John is hardly complimentary, but real anti-Jewish vituperation is found most obviously in the writings of the church fathers, notably John of Chrysostom, Origen, and Tertullian. By the time we reach the greatest of these early theologians, Augustine of Hippo (354–430), we read of "the theory of the witness people." According to this notion, it is not permitted to kill Jews, but it is desirable to make their lives miserable and debased as a living testimony to the fate of anyone who refuses to accept the messiahship of Jesus of Nazareth. A persecuted Jew becomes, then, the embodied witness to a destiny devoutly to be avoided.

The same ideologies, plus the accusation of deicide, persisted throughout the Middle Ages and well into the modern world. But they were applied unevenly, and it is this sporadic application of both anti-Jewish rhetoric and action that leads us to believe that other causes were more significant. Ideological Judeophobia or anti-Semitism has always been available for implementation, at least for the past two thousand years. It emerged, not as a cause, but as a rationalization and a justification of anti-Jewish actions under specific circumstances, especially when crass economic ambitions impelled governing groups toward unseemly anti-Jewish acts. Then, actions that rulers might not otherwise care to admit openly could be disguised and justified with the more intellectual and godly rationalizations of religious theory. Of course, there were extended periods of history when

Jew and Christian or Jew and Muslim lived in harmony. Though Jews were never accepted as social equals, they did business together and fraternized during daylight hours without compunction. Because times were secure and prosperous, anti-Semitism was subdued and mostly private, though the ideology was always available should conditions of social life change.

It is hard to emancipate oneself from the ramifications of this history. It is not an abstract subject, but something that has touched virtually every American Jew within the last century. tsarist persecutions in Eastern Europe began in earnest in 1882, but culminated with widespread pogroms in 1903 and 1905. Nearly 2,500,000 Jews emigrated to the United States from tsarist lands between 1882 and 1924. All of them left their homelands because of fear of persecution, dispossession, confiscation or theft of property, rape, injury, and murder. One of the reasons why they succeeded so admirably in their new home is that there was virtually no chance of returning home, as other immigrant groups had sometimes done. (Roughly two-thirds of all Albanian migrants eventually returned to their homeland! For Jews, it was likely under 1 percent.)

The pogroms of the early twentieth century were followed by Stalinist purges, killings, and the Gulag that continued at least until his death in 1953 and anti-Jewish measures continued until well into the 1980s in the former Soviet Union. To these horrific oppressions, one must add the terrors of the Nazi Shoah and the forced expulsion of Jews living in Arab lands after the creation of the State of Israel in 1948. In other words, for someone my age, anti-Semitism has been an observable reality for my entire life. For younger Jews, it has been the stuff of immediate family history and legend, often passed down by grandparents who themselves fled the brutalities of anti-Jewish persecution.

Unfortunately, our history teaches that those who perpetrated these affronts often justified their actions with Christian symbolism and rhetoric. In my mid-seventies, it is hard not to be aware of the legacy that members of the majority or host culture were perpetrators of anti-Jewish violence, usually supported by their religious faiths. Thus, it is difficult to enter a Christian setting and to see the cross or the crucifix without hazarding a slightly negative reaction. After all, this symbol which has so many positive associations to Christians, nonetheless represents past terror, oppression, and persecution in a Jewish context. The frisson of excitement and thrill that passes through the body of a Christian in the presence of a cross is often replaced by an equivalent shudder of latent anxiety in the mind of a Jew.

Perhaps the hardest conversion to undertake is to recognize that America is fundamentally different from Europe—and certainly from the Europe of past centuries. Even during the colonial period of our history, when there were never more than 2,500 Jews living in the entire British North American colonies, accounts of anti-Semitism are minimal. All of the colonial American universities taught Hebrew, along with Greek and Latin. In 1638, Harvard sought to engage a teacher of Hebrew, provided that he would be a Christian. Judah Monis, a Jew, applied for the position and was hired; it is possible he converted. Aside from training American young men to read the sacred books in their original, the college also was preparing them as missionaries to the Indians. And, since many Christians believed that the Native Americans were descended from the lost ten tribes of Israel, it made sense to prepare these ambassadors to converse with them in the proper manner! Ezra Stiles of Providence, RI had an extensive Hebrew library and always welcomed Rabbi Hayyim Carigal when the rabbi stopped off on his way to or from the Caribbean. There were certainly electoral laws that made it impossible for a Jew to serve in a position of public trust and "blue laws" that mandated that businesses be closed on Sunday (a double day of rest and, therefore, economic disadvantage for those who were sabbatarians). But these were of the nature of minor inconveniences, compared to the generally warm welcome for any new resident who would contribute to the development of the New World and its economic and social health. In a community that was striving to grow, there was little room for intolerance and exclusion; every able-bodied person was needed and, therefore, welcomed.

It may be arguable, but I would hold that there are two documents that have been critical to Jewish survival and success in the United States. The first, of course, is the Torah. Its influence is certainly not restricted to the U.S. It has been the cohesive force and motivation that has made it possible for Jews to survive through the centuries in a wide variety of situations and locales. The second document is uniquely American: the U.S. Constitution and, in particular, its First Amendment's provisions on religious free exercise and establishment. The Bill of Rights (The first ten amendments were adopted in 1791.) applied only to federal issues until the Fourteenth Amendment extended constitutional guarantees to state matters after the Civil War. These abbreviated guarantees of the separation of church and state assured Jews that they could live openly as Jews in this country without any disabilities or restrictions.

I am under no illusions that Jews were any more popular than other dissenting religious sects in the United States or that anti-Semitism had disappeared. But the Founding Fathers had structured this society so that no one religious community was privileged at the expense of any other. For the first time since Jews had lost sovereignty over the territory of Judea, nearly two thousand years before, they were vouchsafed the right to live their individual and collective lives on an equal footing with all other citizens of the nation. And so they came to these shores, slowly but steadily. From the 2,500 who resided in Eastern seaboard cities at the time of the Revolutionary War, the Jewish population grew to 50,000 by 1840 and then tripled to 150,000 just prior to the Civil War. Most of these newcomers arrived from Germany and lands adjacent to it; they came, not to flee anti-Jewish persecution, but in search of expanded economic opportunity. Jewish settlements were found in virtually all the cities and towns where Jewish communities continue to exist today—with the exception of south Florida and a few other places. Jews followed the westward migration of the American population, platted cemeteries, established synagogues, and, most of all, built their businesses in nearly every corner of the country. They were able to do this freely and without hesitation because they were guaranteed that right by the Constitution.

For the four years beginning in April 1861, the nation was convulsed by a brutal and nearly ruinous Civil War. Simon Wolf in his book *The Jews as Citizen and Soldier* as amplified by a number of monographs and articles suggests that Jews repaid the hospitality of both the Union and the Confederacy by serving in the military forces at a rate higher in proportion to their population than the citizenry at large.[1]

The America these immigrants had discovered was, indeed, different from the Europe they had left. In their old countries a conflict that ripped apart the fabric of society would surely have been accompanied by outbreaks of anti-Semitism. Jews would have been caught between the warring parties, and their lives would have been made even more miserable than before. That this generally did not occur in the United States was a remarkable novelty. That three Jews could serve as cabinet-level officers in the Confederacy is even more striking; that would never have happened in Europe. There was one major incident of prejudicial behavior. In 1862, General Ulysses Grant issued General Order 11, which peremptorily expelled all Jews as a class from the territory governed by the Army of the

1. Simon Wolf, *The Jews as Citizen and Soldier* (Philadelphia: Levytype, 1895).

Tennessee. Jews were accused of trading and profiteering with the enemy, and some probably were. But Grant's Order blanketed all Jews, not just those who had violated commercial regulations. A delegation led by Cesar Kaskel left Evansville, IN by train, arrived in Washington, and proceeded to the White House. There, they secured an audience with President Lincoln, made their case and were gratified when the President directed that GO 11 be revoked immediately. There were other incidents (a major anti-draft riot in New York City and a controversy about whether rabbis could serve as military chaplains), but none of them rose to any level of significance for the welfare of America's Jews.

It remained for the period following approximately 1890 for the relationship of Jews and the general population of America to change. By this time, a new flood of European immigrants had begun to arrive on American soil. These immigrants, however, were not from northern and western Europe, the areas from which most prior immigration had stemmed, but from Eastern Europe and the Mediterranean. They brought with them very different cultural traditions and values, not the least of which were two religious faiths that had not been widespread in this nation previously: Catholicism (both Roman and, especially, Orthodox) and Orthodox Judaism. The earlier arrival of Irish Catholics after the Potato Famine of the 1840s had evoked some anxiety concerning a takeover by Papists, but, after all, these were still people from the British Isles. The earlier settlers could feel some sense of commonality and comfort with them. The new Italians and eastern Mediterraneans were significantly different in many ways, as were the Jews who arrived from tsarist lands. A spirit of xenophobia began to sweep through the nation, enhanced by Frederick Jackson Turner's contention that the frontier was now closed and no empty space remained to absorb a new populace and by the pseudoscience of eugenics that proposed that character and personality traits were associated with national, ethnic, physical, and cultural attributes. Depression, unemployment and other economic difficulties furthered the trend as America entered full blush into the industrial era; the arrival of masses of laborers who would work for low wages did not make them popular.

The early decades of the twentieth century witnessed new efforts to enact admission quotas at elite universities to limit the number of "undesirables." Signs began to appear at places of public accommodation and resorts that restricted admittance to Christians and whites. Neighborhood covenants frequently included a restrictive clause forbidding the sale of property to unwelcome prospective residents. Corporations, such as the Ford Motor Company and Proctor and Gamble, adopted informal policies limiting the employment and advancement opportunities of non-whites and non-Protestants. Social clubs closed their doors, and hate groups, such as the Ku Klux Klan, found new popularity. For immigrants, especially those who were culturally and religiously different from the majority and who survived at the bare margins of subsistence, this was a particularly difficult time.

The xenophobia of the era found expression in public policy as the laws governing immigration were tightened. In particular, the Immigration Act of 1924 (the so-called Johnson-Reed Act) established the notion of national quotas; in each year, the U.S. would admit a maximum from each country of no more than 2 percent of the total American population who had roots in that country. Thus, if there were 250,000 "Germans" living in the U.S., the annual quota would be capped at 5,000. The year chosen as the baseline for the calculation of the quota, however, was the 1890 U.S. Census, a year chosen deliberately to understate the number of certain new immigrants because it preceded their mass migration. The Act of 1924 represents anti-Semitism, anti-Catholicism and racism rolled together in action.

Gathered as they were in urban ghettoes and living under abysmal conditions of poverty, disease and exploitation, these were decades during which dual contradictory forces played upon these people. On the one hand, many reasoned, it made sense to acculturate to American mores as speedily as possible. Eliminating the stigma of "greenhorn" by Americanizing implied a possible escape from the negative attitudes that were directed toward the alien newcomer. On the other hand, however, the centrifugal force of acculturation was countered by a centripetal force that reminded immigrants that the only real source of support they could count on was their own immigrant community. Leaving that community behind involved setting out on one's own course, a risky and tenuous decision. The solution was to move from impoverished immigrant into the middle class, but to relocate from the ghetto to a new residential enclave populated by people of similar ethnic and religious identity.

During the stressed times of the Depression of the 1930s, anti-Semitism in the United States reached a new level of vehemence. Individual hate-merchants, like George Lincoln Rockwell and Father Charles Coughlin of the Catholic Shrine of the Little Flower in Detroit, held public rallies, published anti-Jewish literature and spoke regularly on the radio. Jews, many of whom had emigrated from Russia, were identified as Communists, and an international Jewish conspiracy was blamed for the ills that the American population was suffering. This scapegoating was actively encouraged by the German-American Bund after 1933 when its patron, Adolf Hitler and his Nazi Party, gained power in Germany. In surveys taken just before the outbreak of WWII, Anti-Defamation League pollsters reported that roughly half of all Americans were prepared to declare openly that they did not like or trust Jews.

In the 1930s, Henry Fleischman, son of a prominent German-Jewish, elite family, decided he had had enough of anti-Semitism. He went to Cincinnati's very prestigious Hyde Park Methodist Church and studied for conversion. Following his ceremonial acceptance and baptism, he applied for membership in the church. He was refused because, as he was told, "We don't accept Jews."

When American entered the war, however, and the pre-eminent purveyor of anti-Semitic hatred became the enemy, this picture changed almost overnight. Father Coughlin was silenced by the Church, and the Bund ceased its operations. Overtly espousing anti-Semitism made one appear to be in league with the Axis Powers, a decidedly unpatriotic stance. By the time that the horrors of the Nazi concentration and death camps became widely known, far fewer Americans wanted to be associated with the evil consequences of anti-Semitic hatred.

By the turn of the twenty-first century, polls showed a decline in anti-Jewish sentiment from the pre-war's 50 percent to less than 20 percent of respondents. Attitudes toward all racial and religious minorities and toward women had softened, though prejudices were still apparent in some sections of the population. Twenty percent of three hundred million Americans means that there may still be as many as sixty million people who harbor anti-Jewish sentiments. But the society has changed, and only a tiny fraction of them would ever consider actuating their biases into open discrimination or attack. America in the last half century has become more open and accepting of differences. As a symbol of this shift, one might cite the 1954 book by Will Herberg entitled *Protestant-Catholic-Jew* in which he maintained that American Jews represent one of the three basic religious faiths of American society.[2]

2. Will Herberg, *Protestant-Catholic-Jew: An Essay in American Religious Sociology* (Garden City, NY: Doubleday, 1995).

For the past 2700 years, Jews have generally lived as a minority community in a host society that often barely tolerated them. In 587 BCE, the Babylonians under Nebuchadnezzar captured the area of Judea and took 90 percent of the Jewish population into Mesopotamian exile. While they were there, the prophet Jeremiah (29:7) counseled them "to seek the welfare of the city to which I [God] have exiled you and pray to the Lord in its behalf; for in its prosperity shall you prosper." Since that time, Jews, wherever they lived, have included a special prayer known as *Hanoteyn Teshu'ah* in the Shabbat morning Torah service, asking God to bless those in governing roles and pleading for their welfare and for their beneficence toward the Jews who lived under their rule.

We have prayed that the officers of the government live long and prosperous lives and that they be inclined by benevolence and kindness toward their Jewish subjects. None of this was altogether altruistic. We knew from bitter experience what would happen when the ruling elite turned against us. So, we hoped to dwell securely wherever we resided because we recognized, as Italian Renaissance Rabbi Azariah de Rossi (1713–1578) said: ". . . in their peace we too have peace."[3]

For most of Jewish history, the fate of Jews hung uncertainly on the whim of the ruler and the welfare of his society. In a modern idiom, we say the same thing: "A rising tide raises all boats"—ours included. Even in America, where Jews have lived a more secure life than in any previous place, we too invoke divine blessing upon the nation and "those whom the people have set in authority . . . [because they] are entrusted with our safety and the guardianship of our rights and our liberties."[4]

Despite some bumpy roads along the way to the present and despite the continued existence of all sorts of prejudices in America, it appears today that anti-Semitism is no longer associated with mainline Christianity. Some fundamentalist Protestant sects maintain a posture of exclusivism, but a more general observation today would be that Jews have been largely integrated and accepted into the mainstream of American society. The anti-Semitism that was ubiquitous and systemic in Europe still exists on this side of the Atlantic, but only as a fringe and sporadic phenomenon. The bottom line is that America, from its first years until now, is different from any other place Jews have lived in the last two thousand years.

3. Azariah de Rossi, *Me'or Enayim* (Mantua: 1573–1575).
4. *Union Prayer Book II* (New York: Central Conference of American Rabbis, 1973), 85.

It is worthwhile to look at a sample of the experiences that permit me to make this general statement. In both Madison and Corpus Christi, I have met regularly with Christian and Muslim clergy for conversation, common purposes, and mutual support. These sessions have been characterized by open dialogue and considerable humor. Six of us were sitting in the cafeteria at Madison General Hospital when a harried Catholic priest joined us. "I just did something completely contrary to Church practice," he exclaimed, "but I had to do it." A young woman from his parish was upstairs, about to give birth to a stillborn infant. Her very pious mother believed that the child would reside permanently in purgatory unless it was baptized before it was delivered. To assuage the grandmother's grief, the priest arranged to baptize the fetus in utero, an act which he knew violated standard Catholic theology, but which he could justify on compassionate grounds. After a few jocular comments, the group turned to me and wanted to know if the mother had been Jewish would I have done a circumcision in utero. It was this easy and unself-conscious banter that could only have happened in this country. America is different.

Also in Madison, Rev. Lowell Mays, head of the Department of Human Ecology at MGH, showed up at my office one Monday morning. He presented me with the Sunday program from the Lutheran church he and his wife attended. "Look at the anthem they sang after the sermon," he chortled. And there it was in black and white: "Make a *goyful* noise unto the Lord." Only in America would a Lutheran pastor want his rabbi friend to share a belly laugh over such a misprint.

In Dallas, four churches of different Christian denominations and our temple shared a common service the evening before Thanksgiving day. This practice had begun in 1985. Father Katinas once asked the three other ministers and the rabbi to help distribute Holy Communion. But in Corpus Christi, the Episcopal Church of the Good Shepherd and Temple Beth El have been thanking God together since November 1934. At that time, it was so unusual for Jews and Christians to worship jointly that *Time Magazine* actually ran a national news story about the service. These were the early years of the Nazi terror, and the two congregations and their clergy wanted to make a statement that interfaith amity is possible, that prejudice in un-American and that America is different.

Dallas was also the place where our synagogue and a host of churches joined together as Dallas Area Interfaith, an organization intended to empower otherwise marginal people based on the philosophy of Saul Alinsky and his Industrial Areas Foundation. Out of this association came one of my most special friendships. Charles Stovall is an African-American Methodist minister; his small church was in far south Dallas. In 1992, when South Africa voted to elect Nelson Mandela as its first black president, Charles was asked to be one of the election observers. Our congregation helped him with some expense money. Upon his return, he reported from our pulpit, and we then regularly exchanged preaching roles. But one morning, I received a call from him. He posed a question I would never have imagined hearing from a minister. "Ken, I just bought a VW car. But I got to thinking. I come to Temple Shalom often, and I don't want a German car to offend your members if I park it in your lot. I have three days during which I can return the car. If you think it will be a problem, that's what I'll do." I was touched and moved beyond words. When I finally got hold of my emotions, I replied: "Charles, it's not going to bother anyone. Next time you're here, look around. You'll see German cars and Japanese cars and maybe even a few Italian cars! We've learned to move forward, even as we keep the bitter memories alive. America is different."

One more anecdote. I serve on the Development Foundation Board of the Christus Health System in Corpus Christi. Karen Bonner, the executive of the foundation that supports this large Catholic medical complex, called and asked if I could see her. When she got to my office, she laid out her problem. They wanted to create a ceramic plaque that could be presented to board members at the conclusion of their term. The design that had been suggested focused on a large cross at its center, not surprising given that the Sisters of the Incarnate Word sponsor the Spohn hospital. "But I can't use that design," Karen said. "We have lots of Christians on the board, but we also have Jews and Muslims and atheists. I need something that would be appropriate for all our members, not something that only fits for some. Can you suggest an alternative?" Again, I was nearly overwhelmed by the openness and sensitivity inherent in her request. I offered a phrase from the prophet Jeremiah, "Heal me, O Lord, and I shall be healed," and she thought that might be suitable. I don't know if the plaque was ever made, but I treasure the memory of the executive of a Catholic institution coming to a rabbi for help in designing a logo of appreciation. Only in America could this happen. Our society really is different, perhaps unique.

To emancipate oneself from the lessons of the past and to accept the difference that America represents requires an emotional and intellectual commitment and effort of a significant nature. It's not easy to dismiss nearly intuitive reactions to two thousand years of experience. Yet those experiences and the messages that they have conveyed to us are not intuitive; they are learned responses, and it is possible to learn different responses. The challenge of American society, with its opportunities for a different relationship between Jews and other Americans, between one religion and all others, between one culture and other cultures—that challenge is to create a new paradigm for intergroup relations based on mutual respect and trust. My assessment is that this reconceptualization is well on the way to fruition.

9

The Head and the Heart: Intellect and Emotion

THE LEGACY OF CLASSICAL Reform Judaism is a mixed blessing for someone like myself who emerged from that background. On the positive side, one can count at least three virtues that are incontrovertible.

First, there is a fundamental pride in one's Jewish identity. As much as the proponents of the Classical style wanted to be accepted by their gentile neighbors, especially during the period between the two World Wars, they never shied away from a fulsome acknowledgement of their Jewishness. To be sure, their definition of what it meant to be a Jew was different from other Reform Jews and worlds away from traditional Jews, but it was ever a positive identity. For those who could not make this positive affirmation, conversion to Christianity was the alternative option. But most stayed and were proud that they were Jews. The Classical Reform Jew believed with consummate faith that he or she had the ability to make a difference for good in human society and that this blessing derived directly from biblical and Jewish teachings.

The contribution that Classical Reform Jews were poised to make emphasized the ethical and moral teachings of the biblical prophets, as mediated, of course, by the exigencies of history and modern society. These paragons of social progress led reform movements in civic governance, often ousting bosses and corrupt political machines, and initiated any number of social welfare programs that have morphed today into mainstays of the "safety net." Our modern Social Security system originated in large part as an emulation of Jewish mutual assistance societies called

Landsmanschaften. The cottage system of caring for orphaned children began as an upgrade for large Jewish orphanages in the early decades of the twentieth century. Visiting nurses, visiting homemakers, school nurses and pasteurized milk supply emerged from the needs, especially in the Lower East Side of New York and other urban areas of concentrated Jewish population, to keep families together, to offset the ravages of parental death and desertion and to counteract the prevalence of serious illness. Uptown Classical Reform Jews brought these initiatives downtown as "Lady Bountifuls"; they were motivated by a Jewish sense of obligation to their less-fortunate brethren. Though one may, in today's world, decry their self-image of *noblesse oblige*, it is still beyond question that their efforts to make real the ethical mandates of Israel's prophets led to immeasurable constructive results among the immigrant population. It is probably not too much to claim that the relatively rapid movement of immigrant Jews from Central and Eastern Europe into the American middle class was greatly facilitated by the Classical Jewish elites. This propensity toward social activism was a direct parallel of the Social Gospel movement in liberal Protestant circles of the same era.

A third aspect of their legacy that bore positive fruit was the emphasis on the rational dimension of Judaism. They espoused rationalism in part to distinguish themselves from the Orthodox ("anti-rational") immigrants who crowded into American cities between 1882 and 1924 (about 2,500,000 individuals). The lifestyle of these new arrivals conflicted with the acculturated, Westernized, and sophisticated image Classical Reform Jew strove to cultivate, and they wanted to make sure that their neighbors did not confuse them with the newer immigrants. They identified Hebrew, Yiddish, chanting, *davening*, ritual garb and practice, kashrut, Zionism, and ethnicity, and a host of other phenomena as outdated emotionalism of which they would have no part.

An emphasis on ethical and moral values, on social activism and on rationalism marked the high points of the Classical Reform Jewish expression. There is an undoubted sense of pride that the scions feel as descendants from this legacy.

The wake of Classical Reform Judaism that washed up on our contemporary shores, however, was a mixed blessing. I cannot begin to count, for example, how many of its devotees have told me with intense seriousness that Judaism "does not believe in heaven and hell," or that "we do not believe in a messiah." Anyone who reads the totality of the Jewish tradition cannot with integrity make such statements. One can say "*I* don't believe . . ." but one cannot assert that there are no such options for belief in the traditional literature. The vaunted rationalism of Classical Reform was not matched by widespread intellectual achievement within a Jewish context. Virtually the entire medieval rabbinic tradition was neglected and demeaned as a corruption of the original and much-to-be-lauded spirit of biblical Jewish religion. The great intellectual lights of European liberal Judaism, such as Zunz, Geiger, and Baeck, knew the tradition, but they had grown up in Orthodox environments. American liberal rabbis and scholars who had studied in Europe were also aware of the teachings that bridged antiquity and modernity. But this kind of learning generally did not filter down to the laity. Instead, rabbis like Emil G. Hirsch and Louis Mann of Chicago's Sinai Congregation specialized in the delivery of book review and current-affairs sermons intended to help foreign-born Jews and their children learn how a sophisticated and cultured American ought to think and speak. A sermon delivered by Hirsch in 1891 entitled "The Education of Orphans" contains not one word about the extensive history of Jewish communal care of dependent children over the previous two thousand years. It focuses instead only on the modern day problem of orphanages and the need of Chicagoans to make better provision for the children of their city—a laudable topic—but offers no Jewish context or depth that the congregation could carry away for the enrichment of their Jewish knowledge.[1]

Of equal negative import was the dismissal of emotional expression in the practice of Classical Reform Judaism. The worship that was practiced by devotees of this style of Judaism involved prayers in the vernacular because they believed it important that the meaning of the words be clear and comprehensible. One could not accomplish this objective with the rhythm of a Hebrew chant. The congregation occasionally stood up, but mostly sat and never swayed, leaned or genuflected, even during the English version of the *Aleinu*, where the *Union Prayer Book* called on the assemblage to bow their heads but not to bend the knee or incline at the waist.

The conduct of Classical Reform worship was the province of professionals who were good at what they did; laity were implicitly encouraged to respect their skill and avoid interfering with their performance. I have attended services in such temples and have occasionally been moved to sing along with the choir. Most of the time, my vocalizations have been

1. Myron A. Hirsch, ed., *The Jewish Preacher: Rabbi Emil G. Hirsch* (Naples, FL: Collage, 2006), 131ff.

met by glares from other congregants whose message was clear: Your job is to listen while the professionals sing; they know what to do better than you, so your participation in worship is altogether discouraged. Synagogue architecture emphasized the remove of the congregant from the sancta of the religion and enshrined the distance between actors and audience, between rabbi/cantor and member. I have attended services occasionally in one temple where most of the room is in semi-darkness, while a skylight beams bright rays directly on the person conducting the service. Carrying the Torah around the congregation so that individuals could reach out and connect with the sacred scroll never happened. To do so would have involved reducing the distance between the pulpit and the pew, between competent professional and less-than-competent lay person. This and other forms of movement and participation would reduce the dignity and decorum which were the necessary ground of Classical Reform Jewish worship and its identity.

Classical Reform Judaism, however, is largely an anachronism on today's American-Jewish scene. There are certainly temples where this style survives and even thrives to some extent, but a comparison of what goes on even in the services of these sanctuaries and what happened fifty years ago would reveal a vast gulf of difference. A Classical congregation today is a far different place from a Classical congregation two generations ago. What this points to is a basic insight of Reform Judaism: religion, like all other elements of life's experience, is a developmental process. Judaism of any sort grows and changes over time, and any objective observer would see this process at play, even among those ultra-traditionalists who strive to fixate their Jewish practice at some benchmark era of the past. As a Reform Jew and as an historian, I enthusiastically subscribe to the paradoxical proposition that the only constant in the entire history of the people and its religion is change.

Change happens not only to institutions and beliefs, but also to individuals. If I look back at my own life, I observe that in many ways I am not the same person I was a few decades ago. In fact, I have grown, matured, developed, gained new skills, but also abandoned some things I once held dear. My physical self is different than it once was; my hairline has receded, but my waistline has not. Such are the benefits and indignities of the passage of time. But had I not changed, had I remained the same today as I was as a younger man, I would be furious with myself. To be fixated in one place without development would drive me crazy, because the only entities that do not change are those that are dead, either physically, spiritually, or intellectually. So I gladly embrace novelty and fervently declare that the definition of a good day is when I learn something new.

The trajectory of my life testifies to this process. I have tried to chronicle a bit of this in the chapter on "Building a Career." I like the challenge and the risk of taking on a new opportunity for learning, whether it is teaching a new course at the university or becoming the rabbi of a new synagogue or simply trying to make sense out of a situation I had not mastered previously. Simply put, change keeps me alive. So, when in my mid-sixties I had to learn how to conduct a more traditional Jewish service, I welcomed the chance to stretch and to grow. I am still more comfortable in and accustomed to a Reform Jewish service, but, like the crossword puzzles that I complete every day to improve my vocabulary, liturgical and other changes testify to me that I am still vital and vigorous.

The rationalism to which we refer grows organically and authentically out of a very long tradition of Jewish intellectual striving. It was widely acknowledged that the period of direct revelation and prophecy ended about two centuries before the onset of the Common Era. This concept is summarized in the Babylonian Talmud (*Baba Metzia* 59b) with the statement that "From the time that the Torah was given, we do not listen to heavenly voices." From roughly 200 BCE and thereafter, the normative way for Jews to ascertain the will of God was to repair to the authoritative texts of the tradition, pore over them intently and vigorously debate their meaning and application.

If this was to be the *modus operandi,* however, there was a necessary corollary: members of the community had to be provided with basic literacy skills. If one was to be a competent Jew, one had to be able to read and write and, perhaps, do elementary arithmetic. The children of the affluent could afford their own tutors and private instructors. The author of *The Wisdom of ben Sirach* [also known as *Ecclesiasticus*] in the Apocrypha was just such a pedagogue, and a large part of his book summarizes the lessons that he offered his students. There, we confront the values, virtues, and skills a young gentleman from Jerusalem's elite was expected to exhibit as he emerged into adulthood.

But for the children of the average family, private schooling was no more affordable then than it is today. Yet they, as much as their wealthier peers, were expected to be able to negotiate a text. This was true during the late Temple period, when the Torah served as the constitutional law of the commonwealth and violation of its provisions could occasion severe penalties; one had to be able to read the law if one was to be law-abiding. It was even more true after the destruction of the Temple in 70 CE, when a democratic rabbinate replaced a hereditary priesthood. An illiterate had no access to the newly created leadership class. So, even as early as 75 BCE, Shimon ben Shetach initiated compulsory elementary schooling for all male children. Joshua ben Gamla (ca. 64 CE) intensified the process (see Yerushalmi, Ketuvot 32c, and b. Baba Batra 21a). The education of children was considered of such importance that classes were not to be interrupted, even for the rebuilding of the Temple (b. Shabbat 119b). Akiba ben Joseph, who became one of antiquity's most renowned rabbis, began as a poor country bumpkin who plastered himself on the skylight of a school to learn what he could not afford to pay for. He rose through the rabbinical ranks because of his learning, wisdom, and piety (Avot d'Rabbi Natan 12).

From those early times until today, high status in the Jewish community has usually been accorded to the intellectual elite. Whether one was a Talmudic scholar, a Bar Mitzvah boy who delivered a stellar oration or even Tevya, who could "pose a question that would cross a rabbi's eyes," the *lamdan* or learned person was invariably honored far above the *am ha-aretz*, the ignoramus. A rabbinic legend tells of a shipwreck near the Mediterranean coastline. The exhausted survivors swam to shore holding pieces of flotsam, where they collapsed on the beach. Villagers came down to rescue them, but they lifted one man on their shoulders, carried him with dignity to the town, and installed him in dry clothing at the head of a sumptuous table. When the rest of the passengers finally came into town, they asked this man why he had been chosen for such honor. "You are merchants," he declared. "Your goods went down with the ship. But I am a scholar. I have brought my merchandise with me."

When Jews migrated to the United States, they often succeeded in status far faster than their non-Jewish counterparts. I was once asked why this was so. There were a number of reasons, but chief among them was the prevalence of literacy among Jews. *Historical Statistics of the United States* and my own doctoral research confirm that Jews over age twenty at the time of the Civil War were 98.4 percent able to read and write, whereas comparable rates for non-Jews as late as 1870 indicate that about half of the children between ages five and seventeen attended school, but only two percent were high school graduates. Even as late as 1956, less than two-thirds of all Americans over seventeen had completed high school.[2] In an economy that was moving rapidly to focus on occupations that required literacy skills, the difference gave Jews a decided advantage. Even today, it is the rare Jewish high school graduate who does not continue with some kind of post-secondary education, whereas roughly half of all white Americans conclude their education with twelfth grade or less.

The intense Jewish interest in widespread literacy and high rational achievement may have had its unintended advantages in the secular world of economic competition. As a central underlying component of rabbinic Judaism, it led to the creation of serial strata of abstruse works of religious law and thought. From the Jerusalem and Babylonian Talmuds to the medieval commentaries on classical texts and compendia of Jewish practice, to treatises on mysticism to extensive shelves of Responsa, pre-modern Jewish leaders documented the application of the unvarying revelation of Sinai to the constantly changing circumstances of contemporary life. A necessary corollary to the development of the analytic skills required to parse these complex tomes and their often-abbreviated manner of stating the arguments was the honing of a particular form of incisive reasoning. As the emancipation of the nineteenth century opened new avenues of professional endeavor to Jews, the thought process that was initially intended to facilitate rabbinic debate and decision very likely encouraged Jews of the free world to enter occupations that thrived on a similar style of acumen. Thus, it should be no surprise that Jews became lawyers, psychiatrists, and university professors, just to mention a few of the careers where their chances of success were enhanced by skills learned arguing and analyzing complicated issues.

But advantages are rarely unilateral; they almost always involve negative aspects. So it was with rabbinic rationalism and intellectualism. (As a creation of this system from both ends of the spectrum—family classical Reform heritage, on the one side, and fifty years of professional training and experience, on the other—I can easily recognize the deficiencies of the pattern in myself.) There have always been some members of any Jewish community who, perhaps by reason of limited intellectual endowment or of personal predilection, would never compete in this rarefied intellectual arena. There were always many more Jews who were so preoccupied with

2. *Historical Statistics of the United States: Colonial Times to 1957* (Washington, D.C.: U.S. Department of Commerce/Bureau of the Census, 1960); Kenneth D. Roseman, "The Jewish Population of America, 1850-1860: A Demographic Study of Four Cities." Unpublished PhD diss., Hebrew Union College-Jewish Institute of Religion, 1974.

the day-by-day tasks of survival that they had scant time and even less energy to devote to esoteric rabbinic thinking. But so long as the rabbinic elite insisted on bestowing honor and status only upon those who conformed to their standards of religious success and mastered the requisite intellectual skills, the vast majority of the Jewish populace was deprived of a heightened and positive self-image. They were consigned to a second-class caste whose personal destiny was often defined by decisors in unattainable elite circles.

The rabbinic system of textual analysis of which the intellectual elite were so fond had, however, a major limitation. Beginning with fixed texts (principally the Bible and the Babylonian Talmud), there are only a relatively few major insights one can derive from parsing the text. The most natural consequence of the process is then to begin analyzing the analyses, splitting the hairs and then splitting the split hairs themselves until the entire system verges on casuistry. In Hebrew this preoccupation with the minutiae is called *pilpul*, an exercise that can only interest scholars whose full-time involvement is the elucidation of classical Jewish texts. The average Jew neither knows enough to be involved with this activity nor cares; there are other things in life that are much more important than assessing, figuratively, "how many angels can dance on the head of a pin."

In the middle of the eighteenth century, a reaction to the perceived sterility and elitism of the rabbinic process emerged. We call this movement Hasidism (pietism). It was led by Rabbi Israel ben Eliezer, more commonly known as the *Baal Shem Tov*, "Master of the Good Name," or in abbreviated form the BeShT. He was born in Poland around 1698 and died in Ukraine in 1760.

Hasidism emerged as a corrective to rabbanism. It proposed that the essence of the religious life was not intellectual achievement, but the cultivation of personal piety, ethics, and a passionate connection with God. These virtues were available to the common person, even the unlettered and marginally literate. The Jewish version of a lesson that is taught in many folk cultures tells of a little boy who enters a synagogue where serious older men are praying. He does not know the formal prayers, so he begins to recite the alphabet out loud. The worshippers protest that he is disturbing them, but the rabbi quiets them: "If all he can do is say the letters, don't worry. God will arrange them in the right order." Thus, even the simplest prayer is acceptable to the Holy One if it comes honestly from the heart.

Hasidism represented more than a pendulum-swing correction in the face of the excesses of rabbanism. It was that, of course, but I understand its emergence in historical context as a Jewish exemplification of previous phenomena. On the one hand, Hasidism is a descendant from medieval Kabbalah, Jewish mysticism. While all of the practitioners of this esoteric form of Judaism were impeccably observant of the *halacha*, inherent in these alternative systems was the idea that truth could be garnered from sources other than the traditional rabbinic rational forms of textual analysis. Mystical enlightenment does not depend on parsing a biblical or Talmudic sentence; it can come directly through prayer, meditation, or religious exercises. One adept in sixteenth-century Safed is said to have expanded his consciousness through repeated bulimia and sequential vomiting! Once it became possible to think of religious awareness as derivative of one non-traditional style, it was not too much of a stretch to think of more alternative paths to religious consciousness and practice.

One might also think of Hasidism as an extension of the new, inductive way of thinking that was becoming current in the post-medieval world of John Locke and his contemporaries. In the medieval, deductive system, truth emerged from the logical extension of a general principle; conclusions had to cohere with the overall insight and were indisputable, since the general idea was assumed to be true. The essence of the inductive system, on the other hand, is the single, irreducible datum, the individual. In science, this means that one initiates the search for truth with individual facts and experimental evidence. Discrete data are added to each other until enough is known to permit the construction of a hypothesis. The thought process moves in an opposite direction from what was true in premodern society.

As induction moved beyond science into political and religious theory, the individual became the central focus. Thus, for example, the concept of the individual citizen with a direct relationship to the government emerged from this new method of thinking. This could only happen in a minor way in Eastern European Jewish society, where communal discipline and pressure prevented any widespread outbreak of individualism. But Hasidism did offer an outlet for each individual *Rebbe* and his supporters to forge distinctive and different styles of religious life. Again, once that door was opened, it was only a matter of time until more possibilities were examined.

The shift toward more traditional behavior and attitudes that we observe today was affected by two other factors. The creation of the State of Israel in 1948 occasioned a reconsideration of Jewish ritual in all its phases. Not everything changed, to be sure, but permission was given to rethink what we would do in the synagogue and in the home. Thus, for example, more Reform Jews are determined to serve food, both for public and private events, that will be acceptable to a wide range of Jews. There is an increased awareness of our belonging to k'lal Yisrael, to the entire Jewish people and to the responsibilities this imposes on us.

In the chapter entitled "God and Prayer," I spoke about the difficulty of traditional theism after the Shoah. In his book *Zachor: Jewish History and Jewish Memory*, Yosef Hayyim Yerushalmi suggested that an interest in Jewish history was replacing a similar interest in Jewish theology.[3] In fact, doubts about traditional theism had emerged as early as Spinoza in the middle of the seventeenth century. By the nineteenth century, Charles Darwin could adjust his identity from seminary student to naturalist and eventually to agnostic. Long before the Shoah, it had become acceptable in some circles to express the same kinds of doubt and skepticism as we now take in stride. I believe Yerushalmi was pointing to a real phenomenon. The consequence of this resurgence of historical interest, however, has been a renewed involvement with behaviors that some Jews had consigned to the "dust heap of history." It turned out that they were not nearly so dusty and outdated as their detractors thought; they actually served meaningful and important functions in contemporary Jewish life.

They served in many ways to reconnect Jews, especially American liberal Jews to their roots. It has often been said that the pre-WWII task of Jews in this country was to become Americans. But since 1946, the reverse has been the case, and our purpose has been to convert nearly assimilated Americans into Jews. In the pursuit of this goal, traditional behavior and garb has played a significant role.

When the Hasidic motif is projected into the modern, non-Orthodox Jewish world, it offers considerable support for religious individualism and for a move away from rigid rationalism to the inclusion of emotionalism. Intellectual endeavor, precisely because it is capable of overt, public analysis, is a collective phenomenon. Emotional behavior, on the other hand, is essentially idiosyncratic and individual. Our age impels us to indulge in both spiritual forms simultaneously. Since the end of WWII, we have witnessed the resurgence of traditional forms of worship within Reform Judaism. There is more Hebrew; more people—and not just men—are wearing *kippot* and *tallitot*; the structured music of Sulzer and Lewandowski has been supplemented by a variety of alternative styles; poetry has complemented

3. Yosef Hayyim Yerushalmi, *Zachor: Jewish History and Jewish Memory* (Seattle: University of Washington, 1982).

prose. For someone like myself, reared in the Classical Reform Jewish mode, some aspects of this transition are comfortable while others are perplexing. Fortunately, the individualism of the modern world and of Reform Judaism permit me to adopt those ritualistic behaviors that I find compatible with other values of my life, but also to allow others a different path without any need for a judgmental attitude toward their choices.

Since about 1990, one of the buzzwords of rabbis and laity alike has been "spirituality." When the word began to gain currency, it was inchoate and undefined. But, in a general way, it connoted a kind of "New Age" attitude that was as much a counterpoint to rabbinic rationalism as Hasidism had been at its outset. At the risk of outlining a caricature, the spiritual Jew in the first phase of this spiritual searching often wrapped himself or herself in an oversized *tallit*, chanted a Hasidic *niggun* (syllabic melody without words), meditated, engaged in selected religious practices that brought a sense of inner peace and of nearness to the sacred, adopted exercises of the human potential movement, and generally portrayed herself or himself as a religious or spiritual seeker. The epitome of spiritualism during this time was the "JewBu," a Jew who combined Jewish practice with Buddhism. It was also during this phase of spirituality that the term came to be used as a weapon. Someone who remained committed the earlier rabbinic model might be told "You're not spiritual," and it was always intended as a detraction.

As time passed, spirituality became more clearly understood as the pursuit of the holy, as an attempt to become close to God, but now through a diversity of avenues. Thus, one could express spirituality through social action or through study and, of course, through prayer and meditation. When this broader understanding of the idea became widely accepted, it became easier for the Jew who had previously not been considered "spiritual" to be included in this new fold.

We have thought about the relationship of the head and the heart, but there is one other bodily part that needs to be included in this equation: the hand. A folk adage tells us that "actions speak louder than words." The ancient Jewish version (*Pirke Avot* 1:17) says that "Discussion of a subject is not as important as acting it out." The concept that words are cheap and easy to come by, but actions are what really count is borne out by an Arabic proverb ("A cloud is a promise, but rain is fulfillment") and by another pithy folk saying: "It is good to have a heart of gold, but so does a hard-boiled egg." These age-old truths echo the skepticism that one might more naturally associate with modern inductive and scientific thinking. Obviously, the ancients were more canny than we might at first glance give them credit.

What is the conclusion? The modern liberal Jew needs to become an adept at using both the head and the heart and then allowing both of these forces to motivate him or her to lead a life of committed religious, ethical, and moral action.

10

A Line in the Sand

THE IDIOM "TO DRAW a line in the sand" has a lengthy and venerable history. The first, albeit somewhat oblique mention of the phrase, appears to have been in the Gospel according to St. John (8:6-7) when an adulterous woman is brought before Jesus. He draws a line in the sand (perhaps "writes on the ground") and tells the assembled crowd that "he who is without sin should cast the first stone." No one crossed the line.

For Texans, the *locus classicus* is associated with Colonel William Travis at the Alamo in 1836. According to legend, he drew a line in the sand with his sword and invited those who would defend the mission to cross over. All but one person did, even though they knew that their decision was irreversible and probably fatal. In both of these cases—and in many historical instances in-between—the idiom expresses the notion that this is the point of no return, that people have to make a significant choice and that there are serious consequences and costs implied in that choice.

One might quibble that this image is a rather weak one. If the wind blows or the tide comes in, a line drawn in the sand disappears; it is hardly permanent. Nonetheless, it persists in common usage to mean that the limits of compromise and conciliation have been exhausted and that a choice-point has been reached.

Professionals of all sorts are confronted with such lines during their careers. An attorney may be faced with a potential client who is so unattractive that the case is rejected, even at the loss of a sizeable fee. A doctor may be asked to provide a treatment that is unnecessary or even contraindicated and may decide to send the patient away. What is true of professional life is also the case in everyday family life. We are all confronted from time to time with forks in the road, times when we have to make choices. Parents may need to make such a decision with regard to a child who is addicted to drugs or alcohol; a son might want to play football, but his parents may be fearful of life-altering injury; intimate companions may elect to join a club that seems beyond the financial means of a longtime friend. It is of the nature of human life that we are occasionally presented with situations where we need to choose whether to follow or to stand alone, whether to compromise or hold firm to ideals, whether to make a choice between "either" and "or."

For someone in the clergy, this kind of choice can be more agonizing than for other people because there is a general assumption that the clergy are not only servants of God but also servants of the congregation that employs them. A negative response may endanger the clergy person's job, livelihood, and, therefore, the welfare of the family. What is more, clergy are assumed to be reasonable people, and reasonable people, it is widely believed, can always find a middle ground and a way to resolve differences. Not only do the laity believe this about their clergy, but the clergy believe it about themselves. So, drawing a line in the sand is not an act that comes easily or casually to a member of the cloth. I know about this all too well. My English name is "Ken," which in Hebrew means "Yes." By personality, profession, and even by name, I am inclined to be "Rabbi Yes" and to seek accommodation wherever and whenever it is at all possible. Saying "No" is not a skill clergy learn easily or naturally. Saying "No" so the other person is not offended and may even think you have done him or her a favor is a very special attribute that very few of us master and even more rarely are able to implement.

This chapter of the book will be organized in a very different way. I am going to present five case studies, each of which involves making a fundamental choice. Some of these situations are directly related to a religious environment; others will be more general. In any event, it is certainly possible for every reader to reconfigure each case so that he or she can become the decision maker. Each of the cases has a basis in real-life experience, and none of them are so cut and dried that the outcome is simple. At the end of the chapter, the reader will find an appendix in which I have reported the outcome that actually happened. But the reader is invited first to try to figure out what he or she might have done.

CASE #1—TO SERVE OR NOT TO SERVE, THAT IS THE QUESTION

When I entered my senior year at seminary in 1965, the war in Vietnam was just heating up. A representative of the National Jewish Welfare Board met with the class. He explained that they were responsible for securing an adequate number of Jewish chaplains for the various military services and that they had reached an agreement with our Rabbinic Placement Commission that everyone in the class was expected to volunteer for the chaplaincy. Single men and married men without children would be taken first; married men with children would only be called if there were not enough candidates in the first category. No one would be admitted for placement in any other rabbinic position unless he was excused by the NJWB.

Some members of the class were ready to volunteer at the outset. Others, however, felt that the war was immoral and ill-advised; their scruples told them that, by volunteering, they were supporting an effort that was so wrong that they could not be a part of it without sacrificing their own integrity. Conscience was uppermost as their guide of what to do. There was no need to flee to Canada since, as rabbis, they were no longer subject to the military draft. But the consequences of refusing to be part of the military (even if they did not have to go to Vietnam, as was the case of most chaplains) were obviously very severe. Would refusal to serve be a permanent blot and injury for the remainder of their careers? They could, of course, dissemble and claim physical disqualification or procrastinate and hope that they were not called up.

So, to serve or not to serve, that was the question. If you were to face a similar choice, what would you decide?

CASE #2—SHOULD THE FORWARD STUDENT GO FORWARD?

One of your responsibilities is to supervise graduate students as they prepare for careers in education. Almost all of them find part-time jobs to help pay their bills, and this young man is no exception. He arranges to do some private, in-home tutoring with middle school students in a field that he knows something about—foreign language instruction.

One afternoon, you receive a telephone call from the very upset mother of one of his students. She alleges that your student has made homosexual advances to her son, who is a rather fragile and vulnerable youngster. Her son had reported the remarks and gentle touching on the arms and knees, but said that nothing more happened and that the tutor left the minute her son evidenced discomfort. You meet with your student and ask him for his version of the encounter. Once you have heard his side of the story, you are reasonably convinced that the young boy's report was relatively accurate. Of course, it's the tutor's word against the boy's, since neither you nor the mother was present.

Your calculus includes the fact that this student is preparing for a career that will place him in constant contact with young people. Is it ethical to send him forward in school if you believe he is a potential sexual offender? On the other hand, maybe he has learned a lesson and will not be likely to repeat his unacceptable behavior? Should you derail his career on the basis of suspicion, however well-founded you think it may be?

CASE # 3—SHE'S NOT DOING HER JOB

You have a senior staff member who reports directly to you. Her job entails overseeing a major division of your enterprise. In supervisory conferences, you have asked her to do specific tasks, and she has always agreed, but she never follows through on those requests. To help her improve her performance, you have even asked a consultant from the human resources field to meet with the two of you several times, but she is resistant to change. On the date of a major end-of-the-year function, she was absent without permission; no one knew of her whereabouts. The following week, she admitted that she had attended the out-of-town goodbye party for a friend and that she thought it was better to ask for forgiveness than permission (which she knew would not have been granted). Much of this record could be documented.

At the next meeting of the organization's board of trustees (which had the final say about hiring and firing), you make the recommendation that her contract not be renewed. You had thought the record was pretty clear, but you had not counted on this person's political and social skills; she had developed a cadre of supporters among important board members. These same people were only too happy to use the occasion to embarrass the president of the organization, a woman they heartily disliked. The board met in executive session and then reported to you that they had rejected your recommendation. (Incidentally, some years later, she was fired for financial irregularities.)

You are faced with a difficult choice. The board, for reasons that have little to do with either the merits of your recommendation or your own job performance, has repudiated you. Can you continue to work for the organization under these circumstances? Does your sense of personal integrity not demand that resign in the face of what is, essentially, a vote of no confidence? On the other hand, you are doing a lot of good things in the organization and you don't want to see them stop. You know that your departure for reasons that will never remain secret will seriously damage the organization; some of its key supporters may resign in sympathy with you. On a more personal level, you are perhaps five years from retirement. Do you want to jeopardize you present income and your future pension at this critical moment in your career? What choice will you make?

CASE #4—WHO SHOULD WE HIRE?

A few years earlier, the organization had hired a senior person who was openly gay and in a committed relationship. The personnel committee had already determined that sexual orientation would not play a factor in their decision; they wanted the best person for the job. A few people were not comfortable with this choice and resigned, but the large plurality of the membership stayed, and the committee were satisfied that these minimal losses were simply the cost of making a decision based on principle. In the ensuing years, the choice proved to be extremely felicitous, and the new staff person became respected and even loved.

But now it came time to replace another senior team member. Twelve applications were received, and the committee suspected that at least one of these applicants was also gay. Since there were only five members of the executive staff of this organization, they were concerned that having two gay people might inadvertently convey a message to the public that the organization was becoming a haven of choice for the gay community. Perhaps this would not be a good idea. On the other hand, they were also fully aware that modern employment law and practice prohibited asking about sexual preference.

Two questions: First, was their decision that hiring a second gay person was not a good idea in terms of the organization's image either reasonable or proper? And second, assuming that the answer to this question is positive, how could they implement their policy without breaking the law or current practices—or, for that matter, offending any of the candidates?

CASE #5—MOTHER, DAUGHTER, AND THE BAT MITZVAH CEREMONY

I met with a mother about a year in advance to begin the planning for her daughter's Bat Mitzvah ceremony. She informed me that her daughter was not going to read from the Torah; her grandfather had delivered an ultimatum that he would not come if this young woman read from the scroll. I responded that it was the accepted practice of our congregation that boys and girls were treated equally on the pulpit and that all of them read or chanted from the Torah. I asked if the grandfather was an Orthodox Jew and was assured that he was not. I further explained that the Conservative movement not only allows girls to read from the Torah but ordains women to serve as rabbis. I also told the mother than I had a long history of personal commitment to gender equality and that, since this would be the last Bat Mitzvah of my career, I was loathe to deviate from both congregational policy and personal principle. I asked her to reconsider and asked her to call me after she had thought this matter through, but I did not hear from her. Several months later, I initiated contact and discovered that she was adamant. I quizzed the daughter and found that she would do whatever her mother told her to do. She had no independent convictions in the matter. She was a lovely and talented twelve-year-old who certainly could handle all the normal requirements of the synagogue's customs (*minhag*) as well as any of the other young people.

The lay leadership of the congregation indicated that they would support me in any decision that I made, but that "freedom of the pulpit" meant that the choice rested squarely on my shoulders. So I had to decide whether to let the matter rest on principle, congregational usual practice, or find some acceptable alternative that both the mother and I could accept.

In all these situations—and many more of the same nature—I am reminded of a quote from Jacques Jaujard, Director of the French National Museum that had recently been occupied by German forces in 1941. He said: "There are fights that you may lose without losing your honor; what makes you lose your honor is not to fight them."[1]

So the issue for me and for all professionals is how to resolve issues such as are presented in these five cases with integrity and honor intact. In the appendix to this chapter, I suggest ways to approach each of these situations. The reader may have even better ideas and strategies. The composite of these five outcomes will, however, give you a snapshot of my personality and approach.

1. Bret Witter and Robert M. Edsel, *Monuments Men: Allied Heroes, Nazi Thieves and the Greatest Treasure Hunt in History* (New York: Hachette, 2009), 411.

APPENDIX

CASE #1—TO SERVE OR NOT TO SERVE, THAT IS THE QUESTION

For me personally, this was a moot question because I had already served in the U.S. Army. Right after high school, I enlisted as a private, and, following my tour of active duty, continued in the United States Army Reserve until 1964 when I was honorably discharged. Having fulfilled my military obligation, I could not be called for further service as a chaplain.

Like most of the clergy, I was opposed to the war in Vietnam, and I could certainly understand why some of the graduating students would try to avoid serving in any capacity that would imply their approval of the conflict. In counseling with some of them, however, I asked them to consider the men who were serving in the combat zone, often through no choice of their own, and the women who were in rear echelon positions, the families of soldiers, and others who were affected in devastating ways by the experience. What were their needs and was it not the role of clergy to support them? I could not answer for my students and colleagues as to whether personal principle or service to others was the critical and controlling value, but I made it clear that, had I been obligated to serve, I would have volunteered. For me, the needs of the man getting shot at in a rice paddy thousands of miles from home in a war he did not understand trumped my own convictions. Many of my fellow rabbis agreed.

CASE #2—SHOULD THE FORWARD STUDENT GO FORWARD?

Easy choice! Sexual advances, whether heterosexual or homosexual, toward an adolescent student cannot be tolerated. The student was asked to resign from the graduate school and leave immediately.

CASE # 3—SHE'S NOT DOING HER JOB

In absolute principle, you should resign. But there are both organizational and personal pragmatic reasons why this may not be the right course.

As an alternative, consider telling the president of the organization and the executive committee that you think you have very nearly achieved all the goals you set for yourself when you first took the job. It is now time for a younger person, perhaps with a fresh vision, to take the reins and lead the organization. Give them sufficient lead time before your resignation takes effect (anywhere from one year to three) so that they can find a new person and arrange an orderly transition. Without a confrontation over the board's action, leave the position and, preferably, absent yourself from the organization and the city for a cooling-off period.

A solution of this nature may allow you to leave with your reputation intact and without damaging the organization. But it only works because you are close to retirement age and may be able to arrange an early and dignified retirement.

CASE #4—WHO SHOULD WE HIRE?

You agree with the personnel committee that, since there is already one gay person on your small team, a second one might send the wrong message to the membership and potential members. It would certainly create a conversation that would deflect attention from the primary goals of the organization, and that would be patently undesirable.

You could not overtly ask the candidates about their sexual orientation or even if they are married or have significant relationships. Not permitted. What you do is speak frankly with every candidate and make sure that each of them knows that the organization is not averse to hiring a gay person on staff and that one of the present high-ranking persons is gay. (All the candidates had done their homework and already knew.) You also ask them to consider whether they would find it a career help or hindrance if they happen to be gay and were caught up in a controversial situation. Is that the situation they want to find themselves in as they grow in their professional lives? If they think this might be a concern, you encourage them to call you back and consider whether to continue applying or withdrawing. You assure them that every candidate will receive an equal and full interview and consideration, but the choice is theirs.

One candidate called back and withdrew his name. He thanked the person who called him for the thoughtfulness and for thinking of his welfare. One of the remaining candidates was hired.

CASE #5—MOTHER, DAUGHTER, AND THE BAT MITZVAH CEREMONY

The first inclination is to stick to your principles and refuse to officiate or arrange the ceremony. You have spent too many years working to assure a full and equal place in the rabbinate and in congregational leadership positions for women to back away at the last minute. It feels like you are selling out. Besides, the way the mother makes her case seems incoherent and illogical, and you are not even sure that the threat of the grandfather's non-attendance is real.

On the other hand, the fact that the mother's personality presents a difficult problem does not seem a reason to penalize the child who is, in your estimation, a victim in this situation. Is there not some intermediate compromise that will preserve your principle and still bring this girl to the pulpit for her Bat Mitzvah?

You agree to allow her to lead Friday evening services when, according to the more traditional forms of Judaism that the mother favors, the Torah is not read at all. She can read a selection from one of the biblical prophets. There will be no service for her on Saturday morning, so she will not be caught in a situation where she might be required to do what her mother doesn't want her to do. Like most compromises, you exit the situation dissatisfied but comfortable that you placed this girl's welfare higher on the list of priorities than if you had refused altogether. Maybe she will look back on the event and the controversy as an adult and understand something more about what was at stake.

APPENDIX

In all of these instances, I am reminded of a story about President Harry S. Truman. Whenever he was facing an issue that involved decisions about the business world, he would call in his economist advisors and solicit their counsel. Typically, they would respond by saying: "On the one hand, Mr. President . . . but on the other hand . . ." Exasperated, Truman finally yelled: "Damn it, go find me a one-handed economist!"

11

Can A Reform Jew Ever Be Adequate?

IN A SENSE, ASKING the question immediately presumes a negative answer. But the question is deceptive and, in a way, false. What we should really be asking is whether any Jew of any persuasion can ever be adequate. The Library of the Hebrew Union College–Jewish Institute of Religion in Cincinnati contains over 750,000 volumes dealing with Jewish subjects. I once took my calculator and figured that, if one read one of these books every hour, twenty-four each day, 168 a week, 8736 each year, it would take at least eighty-five years of dedicated effort to read every book in the library—and that's assuming that there would be no more books added during that span of time! In short, this is an impossible task. No one can possibly finish learning about the Jewish people, its past, its literary production, its thoughts, its personalities . . . about all the facets of this experience that one ought to know about in order to feel fully adequate. If the goal is to acquire a complete and comprehensive grasp of the Jewish experience, one is condemned to a lifelong task that cannot but end in failure and an admission of inadequacy.

If, on the other hand, one sets a different goal, the outcome may be more positive. That goal must be established in multiple dimensions. Any Jew (and certainly any rabbi) ought first to gain mastery over the basic components of Jewish life and lore. A fundamental grasp of Jewish religious customs and ceremonies (and an ability to express them in both the vernacular and in Hebrew), an acquaintance with the primary forms of Jewish literature, familiarity with major Jewish thinkers and the problems with which they wrestled, knowledge of the basics of Jewish history and a conceptual understanding of the relationship of Jews and the various cultures among which they resided—all of these form the indispensable ground upon which a Jew who would strive to be called adequate must stand.

The second level of adequacy toward which one might aspire is a specialized grasp of one or more specific areas of Jewish learning. When you stand in the library stacks, you cannot simultaneously reach out and select every volume; the intrinsic limitations of humanness require that you select one book and focus your attention on that subject. So it is with Judaism. Once you have conquered the basics, it becomes imperative that you make a selection and then strive to excel at the topic that you have chosen. Realism and honesty compel a fair assessment of what time, energy, and other commitments may allow and even then may demand that the scope of expertise be narrowed rather drastically. While today's Jewish historian may know something about the broad range of the Jewish experience, he or she may claim adequacy only in relationship to a constricted subtopic of the field. Thus, one scholar might become the world's most competent scholar of nineteenth-century Jewish communal services, while another person might focus on the poetry of the traditional synagogue service. It's all in the setting of goals that the issue of adequacy is determined.

A third issue is the recognition that one is never finished and ought, therefore, to feel a continuing sense of dissatisfaction. A Jew ought always to apprehend a gnawing sense of being unfinished, of wanting to learn and do more, of desperately needing to reach out and take the next book off the library's shelves. Until the messianic future is upon us and assured, our human society will continue to be imperfect and we shall not have remedied the ethical and moral ills that beset us. To that extent, we shall not have proved ourselves adequate to the challenge the biblical prophets placed before us over twenty-five hundred years ago. In a paradoxical manner, the goal of a Jew who wants to feel adequate is perpetually to be dissatisfied with our goals and, even more, with our achievements.

There will be of necessity competing goals within the Jewish world. It appears imperative that one possess enough self-confidence and ego strength to resist the temptation to impose the criteria of one person's (or one movement's) goals on someone else. Thus, it is perfectly legitimate for an Orthodox rabbi to aspire to mastery of the Babylonian Talmud and the performance of the traditional ritual *mitzvot*. It is quite another and very illegitimate to demand compliance with this goal from someone else. But, of course, this presumes a fundamental respect for Jewish pluralism, a virtue that is not always present in the community. Some groups within the

Jewish world presume that there is only one way properly to be Jewish and that Jews who do not measure up to that standard may still be Jews, but inadequate or incomplete Jews. The same is true in certain Christian circles. I once had a leader of a church in Dallas called The Believers' Chapel tell me with a straight face that he and his associates possessed the only correct definition of what it meant to be a Christian and that anyone who did not subscribe to their ideology was both wrong and not a Christian. For people who adopt this philosophy, pluralism is tantamount to heresy.

A fundamental commitment to pluralism requires a secure and well-defended ego. One must be able to say that "I have my beliefs and I am comfortable and confident in them," even at the same time that one accepts the legitimacy of other systems of belief and practice. The existence of acceptable alternatives cannot be threatening. To have this kind of personality structure, which is the ground of all successful pluralisms, is not something that emerges in adulthood, but which emanates from childhood and, especially, from adolescence.

A sense of personal competence and adequacy emerges, paradoxically, from both youthful failures and youthful successes. Virtually all characters in the biblical pantheon are portrayed as having feet of clay. Abraham tries twice to pass off Sarah as his sister in order to protect himself. Jacob and Rebekah enter into an elaborate ruse to hoodwink Isaac. Moses murders an Egyptian. Saul, David, and Solomon are all flawed personalities. They are, in fact, portrayed in very human terms, which means that they err and fail. Very few, if any, people succeed 100 percent of the time. A Hall of Fame baseball hitter rarely succeeds more than a third of the times when he is at bat. Between 65 and 70 percent of the time, he fails, but those failures do not destroy his confidence. Rather, he learns from his non-successes and is convinced that each out can move him closer to the next successful at bat. What helps make this attitude possible is the existence of parents, managers, coaches, teammates, and others who support him when he fails and encourage him to look positively to the future rather than reinforcing the notion that he is a failure and incompetent.

Early adolescence is a fragile time for most young people. They look at their parents and wonder if they will ever measure up to, much less surpass, the achievements of their elders. This is particularly, it seems, an issue in a society that values individual achievement and innovation, as opposed to one in which continuity and the repetition of traditional roles and practices is the rule. Modern societies place more pressure on the individual to excel than more traditional ones, where the group tends to regulate aspirations. The early teen years are generally a time of personal testing when the young person discovers strength within himself or herself to meet challenges or realizes the opposite. That is why Bar/Bat Mitzvah ceremonies in the Jewish tradition are so important. At this time of a young person's life, most challenges are met in a group or team. One is a musician in a band, a soccer player among a team, a scout in a pack or den. Success or failure comes not solely from individual effort but from the achievements of the collectivity. Bar/Bat Mitzvah, on the other hand, is exclusively individual. It involves one (and only one) young person standing before a large congregation of both elders and peers and striving to do something quite difficult. Success in the ceremony (and it is imperative that rabbis and teachers orchestrate a positive outcome) translates into a sense of competency in the face of a difficult challenge. This valuation and strengthening of self generalizes into a sense of overall self-confidence and competency, particularly if it is impressed on the young person in an intentional manner.

Even under optimal circumstances, most young people during their formative years will have self-doubts. This is particularly true for those teens who have high achieving parents and who will naturally wonder if they can ever match the achievements of the preceding generation. With careful thought, guidance and a good deal of luck, however, most young people finally arrive at a set of goals that are uniquely their own and that are appropriate and achievable for themselves.

It is of immeasurable help for any young person to have successful adult models of competency. I was blessed during the formative years of my rabbinate with three such personalities, although I only knew one of them personally.

That person was Nelson Glueck, rabbi, president of HUC-JIR and world-renowned archaeologist. From Dr. Glueck, I learned two basic lessons. In the elevator of the seminary one afternoon, he explained that he would not have made a very good pulpit rabbi. "Ken, it's as important to know what you are not good at as it is to know what you can do well." Dr. Glueck also always made time for his scholarly, archaeological pursuits. A shelf of books testifies to those efforts. I suspect my decision to adopt a project every year (see "Building A Career") stems in no small measure from his example.

The second person in whose shadow I walk is Rabbi Abraham Joshua Heschel. He was born in Poland in 1907, the offspring of a distinguished Hasidic family. He came to the United States in 1940, as a result of an invitation from Dr. Julian Morgenstern, then President of HUC. He taught there for five years, then moved to New York City and a faculty post in the field of ethics until his death in 1972. Heschel's books, *The Prophets* and *The Sabbath*, have been mainstays of my religious philosophy, but especially because he also acted courageously in keeping with his beliefs. The picture of Heschel striding arm-in-arm with Dr. Martin Luther King Jr. in Selma has stayed with me as a reminder that actions do speak louder than words.

When I was appointed assistant dean in Cincinnati in 1966, I wanted to put a picture on the wall behind my desk that would symbolize what I hoped I would stand for. Rummaging through the stored portraits in the HUC-JIR museum collection, I came upon just the right one: a picture of Leo Baeck painted when he was teaching in Cincinnati in the early 1950s. Baeck had been a decorated chaplain in the Kaiser's army during WWI. During the years of the Weimar Republic, he became both a world-recognized scholar and author and the chief liberal rabbi of Germany. However, what made Baeck such an irresistible model for me was the fact that he spurned the chance to save himself by going to England and remained with his people to face whatever fate would come their way. Deported to Theresienstadt in 1943, he taught and cared for the prisoners, providing strength and endurance for many others. No one knows how she or he would react under equivalent conditions of persecution, but Baeck's example of self-sacrifice represents an ideal and a hope that seem an inspiration worthy of emulation.

There have been many other influential people in my life who ought to be mentioned. My father, Dr. Jacob Rader Marcus, Rabbi Balfour Brickner, the assembled history faculty and others at Oberlin College, and a long list of people who influenced me. They are all gone, but to all of them I express a deep debt of gratitude.

Jewish competency requires this same process. It is important for each person to elaborate a destination for his or her Jewish journey, a goal that will stretch that person's efforts and involvements, but which is also possible. Thus, an adult convert to Judaism is probably not going to adopt the goal of becoming an Orthodox rabbi. Of course, there must always be an exception. When I served as dean of the Cincinnati campus of HUC-JIR in the late 1960s and early 1970s, a German-Christian graduate student named Wolfgang Schmidt was admitted to pursue a doctoral program in biblical literature and languages. Over the next several years, he became enamored with Judaism, converted according to the Reform ritual and changed his name to Aharon Schmidt. His evolution continued, however, and he became Orthodox, adopting the name Aharon Shear-Yashuv. Eventually, he moved to Jerusalem and, when last I heard about him, he was the head of a yeshivah in the Old City. For most converts, becoming a well-educated and involved liberal Jewish lay person is a more reasonable and attainable ambition.

One's sense of competency and potential adequacy is enhanced if one has an intellectually consistent and compelling rationale for one's identity. That is not to say that one cannot feel Jewishly self-confident without such a rationale, but it certainly helps.

As a Reform Jew, I am persuaded that the way I think about Judaism is historically accurate and eminently defensible. The essence of my commitment is that Judaism has been historically developmental, that change and novelty represent a continuing constant of the Jewish narrative. There have been and are, of course, themes that have persisted in every Jewish age and place, although different eras of the people's history have witnessed varying degrees of emphasis to them. Thus, for example, the insistence of the early literary prophets (Amos, Hosea, Micah, and 1 Isaiah) on the pursuit of social justice, especially with regard to the less-fortunate of society, became muted in the post-exilic prophecies of Ezekiel, Malachi, and their peers. The same motif was configured as stress on intra-communal charity and mutual assistance during the long Jewish Middle Ages, only to be reborn in twentieth-century America as a crusading fervor for women's suffrage, civil rights, and a host of other communal causes. Similarly, the focus on the Promised Land of Zion took on one form during the Babylonian Exile, then another during the Second Commonwealth. When the Jerusalem Temple was destroyed in 70 CE, this same idea became an ideal to be dreamed of and prayed about in the Jewish diaspora, but was rekindled with the Zionist Movement and then made real with the founding of the contemporary State of Israel.

Judaism, as I understand and practice it, is dynamic and changeful. The religion of the Bible was completely re-formed after the loss of Jerusalem's centrality; institutions and rituals never before contemplated were created. The Rabbinic Reformation that occurred during the first few Christian centuries produced a Judaism that Moses would not have recognized. A Talmudic passage (*b. Menahot* 29b) describes Moses attending the academy of Rabbi Akiba, but failing to understand the lesson. So much has changed since his time that he is lost, until he is told that all of what he is hearing derives from the Torah that Moses received at Sinai. Similarly, medieval biblical and talmudic commentators were necessary because so much had changed since earlier eras that the clarity of the text had been beclouded by the shifting social and cultural realities.

It is possible, of course, to maintain that Judaism is still the religion of the Babylonian Talmud, the oral traditions of which are alleged to have been given to Moses along with the written Torah at Sinai. Some maintain that the prayers of the Orthodox service are unchanged since the hoariest days of Israel's past. One may make these claims, but, to me at least, they hinge on a statement of faith and belief and cannot stand in the face of any serious Jewish scholarship.

That scholarly study of Jewish development descends from a long history of oblique suggestions. Abraham ibn Ezra, the great Spanish-Jewish commentator and philosopher (1099–1167), occasionally interjected the note *Hamaskil Yavin*, "the one with good judgment will understand" as a way of indirectly indicating that there was a serious problem with the Mosaic claims of textual inerrancy. Benedict Spinoza more directly challenged the concept of unchanging continuity during the seventeenth century, but it remained for Leopold Zunz (Germany, 1794–1886) to open the gates of modern scholarly exploration of Jewish development. His works on the history of the Jewish sermon and the liturgy of the synagogue service took advantage of new skills in historiography and philology to demonstrate that the Judaism of successive ages may have built on that of previous eras but that it was not the same. Zunz and his colleagues in Berlin innovated *Die Wissenschaft des Judenthums*, the so-called scientific or non-ideological study of the Jewish past. Rigorously, they applied the new tools of modern scholarship to ancient texts and civilizations, and what they discovered was that Judaism had always been in flux and that reform movements had continually characterized the Jewish centuries.

It is, then, a source of great strength and self-confidence to align myself with a movement that can proudly assert that its basic philosophical commitments are identical with what scholars have shown to be the leitmotif of the Jewish past. This stance of Reform or liberal Judaism makes any claim of adequacy or competency difficult because one knows that tomorrow will always be different and that what exists today may not be enough for the future. That is, however, the nature of the commitment and of the task: never to be smug and self-satisfied, always to be a bit tentative and uncertain, constantly to know that whatever one has become for the present will probably not be sufficient for the days to come.